Kisha,
Thank you for
your support.
Contentment

SHINE
2022

MW00561233

I'M SINGLE,
So What?

A Woman's Journey to Spiritual Contentment

DR. HEATHER E. BURTON

Copyright © 2019 Griffin Scott Press, LLC

All rights reserved. No part of this book may be reproduced, stored, or
transmitted by any means—whether auditory, graphic, mechanical, or
electronic—without written permission of both publisher and author, except in
the case of brief excerpts used in critical articles and reviews. Unauthorized
reproduction of any part of this work is illegal and is punishable by law.

ISBN: 978-0-9897526-5-7 Paperback
ISBN: 978-0-9897526-6-4 Ebook

Library of Congress Control Number: 2019941505

CONTENTS

PART III
WORKING YOUR WAY TO CONTENTMENT

$\mathcal{I}$NTRODUCTION

Quite often, women believe everyday contentment or happiness only occurs for married women or women in committed relationships. As a result, these women spend most of their single season concentrating on how to get a man or being in the wrong relationship instead of finding satisfaction in their single and non-committed phase. This book is written as a blueprint to help Christian single women embrace the truth that happiness is not rooted in marriage or a significant other's validation, rather in finding contentment in being single and building a personal relationship with Jesus Christ.

Someone is always inquiring about my relationship status as a woman; with the conversation usually beginning with, "Are you single?" I think to myself, *Yes, I am, so what? If you are not asking me on a date, what's it to you?* I know many of you deal with this same issue --- that never-ending, elusive quest to determine one's marital status.

If ever I give a reply to the inquiring mind, the conversation inevitably continues with the same follow-up question, "Why are you single?"

My candid response, "If I knew, then I probably would not be single!" Most people struggle with straight-to-the-point, candid answers, and are put off by my flippant reply. However, when it comes to being single, candidness is a necessity on so many levels.

The word, single, automatically means alone, no mate, or significant other. Though, many women are single for various and specific reasons-divorced, windowed, choice, opportunity, etc. Being single can be a conscious or unconscious effort. It could be that you are waiting on God to send you a Godly man, or maybe he did, and you passed up that God-sent man because you were not ready. Whatever your reason for being single, it doesn't have to be justified. It is time for the world (and us) to realize that there is nothing wrong with being single, irrespective of your age. A fifty-something year old woman can own her singleness just as boldly as a twenty-something year old.

Now I know that some of you have no intention of staying single forever. You are praying for that Godly man, that man who has a relationship with Christ, that man who is going to love you like Christ loves the church. Christian ladies, I know; I am that woman too. That woman who believes God has her Boaz right in the next field waiting on me to glean, but until then, I am thankful I have learned how to be gratified and full in single living. I thank God for giving me a peace and joy that satisfies me, even in my current station in life.

In this book, let's talk about the ups and joys of being single. We'll discuss how a Christian woman can find serenity while single. There is a line in the movie *12 Years a Slave*, "I don't want to survive, I want to live." How often have we heard, "I'm surviving"? What does that mean, to survive? As single women, we have to stop surviving and start living.

In the words of Beyoncé, "All my single ladies," it's time to find out what's keeping you back from embracing your singleness and finding contentment in Christ-centered single living.

PART I

A WOMAN'S JOURNEY TO SPIRITUAL CONTENTMENT

CHAPTER ONE

THE FACTS: CONTENTMENT

It had been years since Jennifer's last date, but that didn't bother her. However, it bothered her two friends. They hounded Jennifer that she needed to go on a date. Jennifer always listened to their comments but never acted on them.

"You need a man in your life!"

"Jennifer, what is wrong with you? Why do you refuse to date?"

Their comments didn't bother Jennifer even slightly, because over the years, she had learned how to live a full existence without being in a relationship. There was not a new movie that Jennifer didn't take herself to see. This was a time in her life when she no longer waited for someone, specifically a man, to go out. Jennifer attended plays by herself. She ate at the finest restaurants by herself. She discovered life by not being inhibited and was happy.

Many times, we as Christian women are caught up and blinded by societal labels placed on single women. These labels can also bring about feelings of guilt or shame when we find enjoyment while single. It reminds me of a time I attended a graduation party, and joined others on the dance floor for a line dance. Yes, sisters! This Christian woman line dances! I happened to glance over and noticed a young lady, getting her life and having her own party in her head. She looked to be having the time of her life. The thing that caught my eye was the young woman had Down syndrome, but her disability never inhibited her from having a ball. Unfortunately, as single Christian women we have become bound by our singleness and allowed it to detract from our ability to live a life full of God's promises. It is time for Christian women to live uninhibited, single or not.

To Be Content or Contentious

As I began researching *contentment* and *content*, I came across *contention* and *contentious*, which means the act of contending. But these two words come from the word *contend*, which means to struggle, as in battle. Contention is competition or rivalry, while contentious is quarrelsome. The Bible speaks of contention nine times and contentious five times. I point this out because if we are not keenly aware of specific words meanings, we can easily misuse them in context. At first sight these words can easily be mistaken for a form of the word *content*, but upon closer observation, we learn that *contention* and *contentious* have negative meanings. *"Only by pride cometh contention: but with the well advised is wisdom" (King James Version*, Proverbs 13:10). *"A fool's lips enter into contention" (King James Version*, Proverbs 18:6). *"A foolish son is the calamity of his father: and the contentions of a wife are a continual dropping. House and riches are the inheritance of fathers: and a prudent wife is from the Lord" (King James Version*, Proverbs 19:13-14). *"But unto them that are contentious, and do not obey the truth, but obey unrighteousness, indignation and wrath, Tribulation and anguish, upon every soul of man that doeth evil...But glory, honour, and peace, to every man that worketh good..." (King James Version*, Romans 2:8-10). In this passage of Scripture, the Greek word for contentious is *eritheia*, which represents ambition, self-seeking, and rivalry, with self-will being the underlying context. If a single Christian woman is mistaken for contentious instead of content, she is consumed by strife, jealousy, wrath, and fraction. A contentious woman is consumed by ungodly characteristics that are far from the life of contentment. *"A contentious woman is like the dripping of a leaky roof in a rainstorm; restraining her is like restraining the wind or grasping oil with the hand" (New International Version,* Proverbs 27:15). In other words, a quarrelsome woman is far from content. A single woman that is contentious is bitter, unhappy, and always looking for the negative, unlike the content Christian woman, who is satisfied and experiencing joy in her current state of singleness. *"But godliness with contentment is great gain" (New International Version,* I Timothy 6:6).

Many of us believe that we have a grasp on understanding the word *contentment*. We are certain that we are living our best lives of contentment. But what is contentment, and what does it mean to live in a state of contentment? According to the Webster's Dictionary, contentment means the state of being *satisfied,* "to gratify the need, desire, or expectation of: to fulfill." Contentment means that you are spiritually fulfilled in your current state, mood of existence.

We hear the word all the time, *contentment.* I remember this word being the context of a conversation I had with two friends in college. My friends and I were discussing our future economic status, or what we hoped it would be once we graduated. I had one friend who stated she wanted to be comfortable, content. I said, "For me, being content is being rich." I associated my contentment with the amount of money I wanted. Spiritually growing I now understand that contentment is not based on the amount of money I have but the relationship I have with Christ. I was a babe in Christ, I did not know any better. However, in the words of James Cleveland and Albertina Walker, "Please be patient with me, God is not through with me yet!" Contentment is a spiritual satisfaction in my emotional and mental well-being. The conditions that surround the securing of money contribute to my emotional and mental well-being, my contentment; but not the objectivity of money itself. For instance, the lack of money, which is caused by a negative change in your current economic status, or the abundance of money caused by a positive change in your current economic status (the conditions) is what controls the mental and emotional condition or existence (the state of contentment). Bottom line I've learned that money is not the source of contentment. Contentment is not based on conditions.

Paul Explains Contentment

In Philippians 4:11-12, Paul is satisfied in his mental and emotional condition and mode of existence. Paul pens, *"Not that I speak in respect of want: for I have learned, in whatsoever state I am, therewith to be content. I know both how to be abased, and I know how to abound: everywhere and in all things I am instructed both to be full and to be hungry, both to abound and to suffer need."*

In this passage of Scripture, Paul points out that contentment means that no matter what the situation, we are satisfied in our mental and emotional condition; we deal and adapt without complaining or bitterness. *"Not that I speak in respect of want"*; Matthew Henry's commentary suggests that here Paul is saying that he does not speak in respect of the want he feels or the want that he fears. In reviewing the contextual definition of want—Paul's feeling of want means to desire greatly, while his fear of want references his lack of, to be without and failing to have. In the former Paul was content with the little he had and that satisfied him, and in the present and future he was content because "he depended upon the providence of God to provide for him day to day, and that satisfied him" (Henry, 1960).

As Christians, we must also do as Paul and depend upon the foresight of God to provide day to day and not speak in respect of want, because we should *"Delight thyself also in the Lord; and he shall give thee the desires of thine heart"* (*King James Version*, Psalm 37:4). If we as single Christian women take great pleasure or gratification, even joy in our relationship with Christ, then our words will not be in respect to want because we will have come to a place, a state of contentment, where we understand that Christ provides according to his will and his word.

In 11b of Philippians 4, Paul declares *"for I have learned, in whatsoever state I am, therewith to be content."* This segment is representative of three words that summarize our ability to confirm satisfaction and fulfillment: *learned*, *state*, and *content*. Paul writes, *"For I have learned,"* which means an active search for knowledge or an acquired gain of knowledge through experience. Paul's spiritual contentment was not something he had at the inception of salvation, but after many of life's difficult experiences he learned the "Overruling Providence of God, the Unfailing power of God, and the Unchanging Promise of God" (Wiersbe, 1989).

God's providence means that he sees it beforehand; it does not mean that God simply knows beforehand but it is the working of God in advance to arrange circumstances and situations for the fulfilling of his purposes (Wiersbe, 1989).

The "Unfailing Power of God" means that the power that God possesses never fails. *"He hath made the earth by his power, he hath established the world by his wisdom, and hath stretched out the heavens by his discretion" (King James Version,* Jeremiah 10:12). And because God's power does not fail, the power that he supplies the believer through the indwelling of the Holy Spirit enables that *"I can do all things through Christ which strengtheneth me" (King James Version,* Philippians 4:13).

The "Unchanging Promise of God" is indicative to the promises of God being fulfilled in and throughout his Word. Because God's promises are unchanging, we as Christians can hold truth to the fact of Philippians 4:19: *"But my God shall supply all your need according to his riches in glory by Christ Jesus." (King James Version).* Our source of contentment comes from the fact that we have "learned" the providence of God, the power of God, and the promises of God (Wiersbe, 1989).

"In whatsoever state I am." Paul is saying that no matter what the circumstance, we can find comfort in knowing that Jesus Christ is our Source for day-to-day living. According to the American Heritage Dictionary, *state* means "a condition or mode of being with regard to a set of circumstances; position" (Houghton Mifflin, 1190). As Christians, our ability to emotionally and mentally handle our condition or state must not be a reflection of our circumstances, but a reflection of HIM that controls our circumstances. That means that just as Paul, *"I know how both to be abased and I know how to abound; everywhere and in all things I am instructed both to be full and to be hungry, both to abound and to suffer need" (King James Version,* Philippians 4:12).

Matthew Henry's commentary suggests that to be at this point in life is a "special act of grace, to accommodate ourselves to every condition of life." To accommodate ourselves to an afflicted condition of life means we know how to be abased; to accommodate ourselves to a prosperous condition means we know how to abound. We know how to be full, which does not mean proud and secure in self, but proud and secure in Christ (Henry, 1960). *"Who shall separate us from the love of Christ? Shall tribulation, or distress, or persecution, or famine, or nakedness, or peril, or sword...Nay, in all these things we are more than conquerors through him that loved us" (King James Version,* Romans 8:35,37).

A State of Discontentment

Once we learn the source of our contentment, we immediately begin to recognize when we fall into a state of discontentment. Contentment in Christ is achieved by being able to recognize when our circumstances are leading us to a negative mental, emotional, or behavioral state, and counteract that state knowing that God's hand is controlling the plans for our lives. *"For I know the plans I have for you,'* *declares the LORD, 'plans to prosper you and not to harm you, plans to give you* *hope and a future'" (King James Version,* Jeremiah 29:11). As Christians, we should understand that contentment is found because we have a reassurance declared in the word of God. However, within a worldly connotation, we falsely identify contentment to be in people, places, and things (remember from elementary school the definition of a noun).

As Christians, when we begin to grow in Christ, we learn that contentment is in the promise that God is an omnipotent, all-powerful God. And because God is all-powerful—God is Healer, Comforter, Provider, and Mighty Counselor—this lends comfort to the single Christian woman to aid in her mental and emotional well-being.

When we as single Christian women allow our mental, emotional, or behavioral state to be consumed by negative circumstances, we fall into states of fear, discouragement, loneliness, doubt, confusion, depression, anxiousness. But the word of God says, *"do not worry,* *saying, 'What shall we eat?' or 'What shall we drink?' or 'What shall we wear?'* *For the pagans run after all these things, and your heavenly Father knows that* *you need them. But seek first his kingdom and his righteousness, and all these* *things will be given to you as well. Therefore, do not worry about tomorrow, for* *tomorrow will worry about itself. Each day has enough trouble of its own" (King* *James Version,* Matthew 6:31-34). Understand that contentment does not mean that God will not give us our desires or wants. It just means that you are satisfied until the desires are met by Christ. When we seek after God, our wants and needs align with his will, which then enables us that no matter the circumstances, we remain in a state of contentment because we know God is in control.

The Heart and Mind of Contentment

In understanding contentment, I must point out the roles that the heart and mind play. The heart and mind become the primary premise of contentment because they are a cause and effect of our emotional, mental, and behavioral state due to circumstances.

The word of God indicates the importance of the heart by its reference in the singular or plural 942 times throughout the Old and New Testaments. Heart is mentioned in all 66 books of the Bible except for Amos, Jonah, Micah, Habakkuk, Haggai, Philemon, and Jude. The heart is the nucleus of who Christians are. If our hearts are not right, then our living is not according to the word and will of God. *"That he may incline our hearts unto him, to walk in all his ways, and to keep his commandments, and his statutes, and his judgments, which he commanded our father"* (King James Version, 1 Kings 8:58). Our hearts are a guiding force to our emotional, mental, and behavioral state. For instance, in the words of Al Green, "If loving you is wrong, I don't want to be right." The emotional state of the heart operates on feelings, but as Christians, we must make sure that our states of emotions are in tune with the Holy Spirit, because then it aligns to the will of God. *"And he that searcheth the hearts knoweth what is the mind of the Spirit, because he maketh intercession for the saints according to the will of God"* (King James Version, Romans 8:27). When we encounter the love of Christ within our hearts, we experience contentment, a fullness that keeps us satisfied in every and all circumstances. *"That he would grant you, according to the riches of his glory, to be strengthened with might by his Spirit in the inner man; That Christ may dwell in your hearts by faith; that ye, being rooted and grounded in love, May be able to comprehend with all saints what is the breadth, and length, and depth, and height; And to know the love of Christ, which passeth knowledge, that ye might be filled with all the fulness of God"* (King James Version, Ephesians 3:16-19).

Hezekiah Walker sang, "Flowing from my heart are the issues of my heart," meaning that whatever we emotional, mentally, and behaviorally connect to is what is expressed in our attitudes. Walker says that flowing from his heart is gratefulness, because he's thankful for the things that God has done. However, if your heart is not aligned to the will of God, you will not experience the gratefulness of every situation, positive or negative. Instead, you will have discontentment. *"For where your treasure is, there will your heart be also"* (*King James Version*, Matthew 6:21). The Apostle John points out that because of the indwelling of the Holy Spirit, Christians have a peace that allows us not to be troubled during difficult times. *"Peace I leave with you, my peace I give unto you: not as the world giveth, give I unto you. Let not your heart be troubled, neither let it be afraid"* (*King James Version*, John 14:27).

"Take delight in the LORD, and he will give you the desires of your heart" (*King James Version*, Psalm 37:4). Our hearts dictate not only what emotions flow from it, but it also dictates the flowing of our desires. As single Christian women, our desires must also align to the will of God, which must be in tune with our hearts. So many of us, including myself, had self-willed desires. What do I mean by that? We had desires that are not of God's will but of our will. When the desires of the heart are not of God, it takes us far away from a state of contentment. Having desires that align with God ensures contentment because we do not become sidetracked by those things that cause discontentment, desires of self instead of God.

Our mind is equally as important as the heart in assisting with our contentment. The word *mind* and its word forms (minded, mindful, minding, minds) is used 137 times throughout the Bible. *"Let this mind be in you, which was also in Christ Jesus"* (*King James Version*, Philippians 2:5). Christ had a mind of love, a mind of purity, a mind of peace, and the list goes on and on of the type of mind Christ had. T. W. Hunt writes in his book *The Mind of Christ* that in order to have a mind like Christ, we must strive to have Christly characteristics, such as *"love, joy, peace, temperance, long-suffering"* (Hunt, 43; *King James Version*, Galatians 5:22).

Our thoughts can easily influence our state of contentment. Our thoughts must be consciously placed on Christ in order to stay in a state of contentment because fleshly thoughts will easily lead us to a state of discontentment. *"I thank God through Jesus Christ our Lord. So then with the mind I myself serve the law of God; but with the flesh the law of sin" (King James Version*, Romans 7:25).

The achievement of contentment comes from a heart and mind that is focused on Christ. In a state of contentment, your circumstances are not always explainable or understood, but that does not dictate or hinder your ability to internally experience joy and peace. *"And the peace of God, which passeth all understanding, shall keep your hearts and minds through Christ Jesus" (King James Version*, Philippians 4:7).

I have heard many say that Paul's example of persecution keeps one from wanting to be a Christian, because if Christians must experience what Paul experienced–blindness, persecution, jail, and suffering–because of his belief in Christ, who wants to knowingly face that? But in spite of what Paul went through, Paul gives the Christian believer, especially the single believer, an example of what it means to be content in whatever state.

Although God has not intended for everyone to remain single, there are some chosen Christians God has called to a life of being single; for example, Paul. *"For I would that all men were even as I myself. But every man hath his proper gift of God, one after this manner, and another after that. I say therefore to the unmarried and widows, it is good for them if they abide even as I. But if they cannot contain, let them marry: for it is better to marry than to burn" (King James Version*, Corinthians 7:7-9).

Singleness is a gift from God, as is everything else that we have. However, so often we look at singleness as a negative thing because the world has added so many taboos to the single woman. As single women, let's recognize how much more time we have to dedicate to the Lord and his work. Singleness allows more time to focus on the work and ministry of God.

As we continue to live as single women, we must recognize that there is nothing wrong with being single; instead our mental, emotional, and behavioral well-being are in a state of contentment because of our relationship with Jesus Christ. Single sisters, we must find contentment in our current states of singleness and actively become satisfied with living a life pleasing to Christ. That does not mean that there will not be persecution, trials, tribulations, and lonely nights, but it does mean that just as Paul, no matter the circumstance or situation, we have learned to be content no matter what state.

CHAPTER TWO

A THORN IN MY FLESH

I remember growing up and always hearing the pastor, the preacher, the Sunday school teacher, my mom, refer to something or more so someone as she or he is "a thorn in my side." As a babe in Christ, of course I did not have any idea what they were talking about. When I thought of thorns, I thought of stick-a-bushes and being pricked in the arm on my two or three camping excursions. Every spring the changes in season would bring about a change in my body; sneezing, wheezing, coughing, running eyes, itching—seasonal allergies. Over the years, I have prayed that God remove this thorn. The thorn of seasonal allergies has been replaced by food allergies—needless to say the nagging, constant reminder, bitterness, or thorn of allergies has not been removed, but as Paul, for this moment I live with my thorn. And as I continue to mature in Christ, I have learned through my own nagging experiences of life what it means to have a thorn in my side.

Paul uses a thorn as an analogy.

And lest I should be exalted above measure through the abundance of the revelations, there was given to me a thorn in the flesh, the messenger of Satan to buffet me, lest I should be exalted above measure. For this thing I besought the Lord thrice, that it might depart from me. And he said unto me, My grace is sufficient for thee: for my strength is made perfect in weakness. Most gladly therefore will I rather glory in my infirmities, that the power of Christ may rest upon me. Therefore I take pleasure in infirmities, in reproaches, in necessities, in persecutions, in distresses for Christ's sake: for when I am weak, then am I strong (King James Version, 2 Corinthians 12:7-10).

A thorn is "a modified branch in the form of a sharp woody spine" (Webster's Dictionary, 1148). A thorn is pricklly; it sticks, it cuts, and it's definitely known to hurt. A thorn is nothing but a mere distraction. It causes us to lose focus because we become so in tune to the pain or suffering being caused by the thorn that we lose sight of who is the thorn-soother and remover. Suffering is a natural part of life. Sometimes our suffering comes because we are disobedient to God; other times, because it is life. Suffering is also used to get our attention, as the thorn was used in Paul's flesh to cause discomfort. Because we are joint heirs with Christ and reconciled unto Christ because of our belief in Jesus Christ, we share not only in Christ's glory, but also in his sufferings (Romans, 8:14-17).

So as single Christian women, we will have suffering. Paul suffered! Because Paul was a joint heir with Christ, Paul experienced Christ's suffering and the glory of Christ. Paul was in prison. Paul suffered blindness. Paul suffered ridicule. Paul suffered the loss of friends. Paul suffered! We will suffer!

There are a lot of speculations as to what Paul meant by thorn in the flesh. Some Protestants suggest that the thorn is representative of a physical problem, such as epilepsy, malaria, tuberculosis, weak eyes, etc. While Catholics believe that Paul's thorn was mental or spiritual in nature, a nagging doubt or persistent temptation. Others believe that it was Paul's constant exposure to nagging criticism or persecution (Chafin, 289). Whatever the exact cause of the thorn, we know that it represented something not pleasing in Paul's everyday life, as attested to by the fact that Paul asked to have it removed not once, but three times. Instead of removing the thorn, God gave the reassurance of his grace and reminded Paul that HIS strength was made perfect in weakness.

Paul never came to feel that the thorn in itself was a good thing, believing rather that it was *"a messenger of Satan"* (*King James Version*, 2 Corinthians 12:7). But he did come to that place in his life where he could see how God's grace could transform what was bad into something good in his life (Chafin, 289). As Christian single women, we have to come to a place in life where we realize that our thorns may not be all good, but God's grace can transform the bad into good if we continue in strengthening our relationship with our Lord and Savior, Jesus Christ.

Being a single Christian woman takes work—we must deal with the constant thorns of life, whether physical—not having the body you think you want—or mental, the temptations of the world or nagging doubts of life. God is capable of balancing our lives through the good and the bad. "If we have only blessings, we may become proud; so He permits us to have burdens as well" (Wiersbe, 674). If we lived a life with nothing but blessings, what would grow our relationship in Christ? Think about how often when things are going good, we forget to thank God for his goodness, but it's in times of need, despair, or disappointment that we find our prayer life improving and the word of God being read. Suffering draws us nearer to Christ.

In this passage of Scripture, Paul begins offering a reason for why he has this thorn. Paul explains that because of his previous blessing by God, in order to keep him from being proud, he was given a thorn. He accomplished many things in his ministry, just as many of us who are single have; we have been able to reach great accomplishments in career, personal life, and ministry. However, what He is suggesting is that sometimes because of our accomplishments we get full of pride, and lose sight of where our blessings or strength are from. It is easy as a single woman to get caught up in the idea of "self" because we feel we are in this battle alone. But as Christian single women, we must never lose sight of our Redeemer, the one who gives us life to do HIS work for HIS glory. Paul suggests to believers that in order for us to remember that our weakness is Christ's strength (Romans 12:10), we sometimes have to have a reminder through thorns in the flesh.

Just as Paul, having a thorn in the side does not mean that you are happy or satisfied with it. It just means that you know the suffering is for a reason: to bring you closer to Christ, to keep you from becoming boastful—not a Christ-like characteristic. His thorn was a messenger of Satan. Paul's thorn was a tool of Satan. As Christians, we experience thorns placed in our side by messengers of Satan, or Satan's imps. Those individuals who always manage to bring negativity to and in every situation. Those imps that keep poking you in the side until you become a main player in their drama. You have to be careful in dealing with imps, or Satan's messengers. Always pray and ask God if this person should be a part of your life and why they are in your life, and that means any relationship-friends, boyfriends, guy friends, sister friends, family. Because Paul clearly asks the Lord thrice, or three times, to have the thorn removed, it must have been painful, shameful, or embarrassing. However, the Lord did not see fit to remove the thorn; instead the Lord responded with, *"My grace is sufficient for thee; for my strength is made perfect in weakness" (King James Version,* 2 Corinthians 12:9). From the comforting words of the Lord, Paul said, ok, Lord. *"Most gladly therefore will I rather glory in my infirmities, that the power of Christ may rest upon me. Therefore I take pleasure in infirmities, in reproaches, in necessities, in persecutions, in distresses for Christ's sake: for when I am weak, then am I strong" (King James Version,* 2 Corinthians 12:9-10). Can you take pleasure in infirmities, reproaches, necessities, persecutions, or distress for Christ sake?

CHAPTER THREE

THORNS OF DISCONTENTMENT

In order for a single woman to reach contentment, she must understand what situations or states lead to discontentment. Factors within a single woman's life can lead to discontentment; a new job, a new date, no new dates, no job, children, loss of a loved one. I like to call or label these factors, which are not exhaustive to this list, "thorns." By using Paul's analogy of a thorn in the flesh, one can begin to understand how situations in life can lead to discontentment. Thorns in the flesh are life factors that lead to states of discontentment. Because just as Paul asked the Lord three times to remove the thorn from his flesh, many of us have asked God to remove a thorn in the flesh from our lives, whether it be a person or a situation.

A thorn in the flesh sticks, pokes, and prods us in many different ways. In the next few sections, I will address a few thorns that tend to stick, poke, and prod the single woman into states of discontentment. Fear, loneliness, discouragement, depression, anxiety, doubt, and confusion are a few factors that push single women into discontentment. Not only are these created from situations, but these factors are established through an emotional state.

Remember from chapter one, contentment results when our hearts and minds are aligned to the will of God. When I think about the mind, I think about how many times I have let my thoughts cause a state of discontentment for me, placing my own self-inflicted thorn. It's important to understand that Paul's thorn was not self-inflicted; it was placed as a messenger of Satan—to keep Paul humble. And yes, some thorns are based on uncontrolled life happenings. However, many of our thorns, more times than not, are self-inflicted. We stare out the window to see what tree has the biggest branch and then we walk to that tree, break the branch, and stick ourselves in the side through ungodly decisions and ungodly guidance. As single women, and Christians in general, we must *"pray without ceasing"* as in I Thessalonians 5:17 (*King James Version*). If we begin to pray and consult God about all decisions (everything), we will find less branches hanging out of our sides. I know praying about everything sounds crazy, but Holy Spirit direction keeps us from having ribcages filled with thorns. Some of us, including me, have made so many wrong decisions that both of our sides are full and the pricklies are now covering our backs. We get so ingrained in our thoughts of the "what ifs" that we can no longer focus on the "what is". If we stay in constant prayer and dependent upon the voice of God our minds will not focus on the what if's because the mind will be focused on the blessings or the source giver of the "what is".

I was in a conversation once with a student of mine who was so focused on the "what ifs". Every scenario she gave about her current relationship was a "what if". I have come to realize that the "what ifs" are created because we are in a state of discontentment. The "what ifs" create thorns. The "what ifs" are the fear, the discouragement, the doubt that leads to states of discontentment.

The following thorns focus on the mental, emotional, and behavioral side of discontentment, as some suggest was the cause of Paul's thorn.

<u>Thorn of FEAR</u>

"Have not I commanded thee? Be strong and of a good courage; be not afraid, neither be thou dismayed: for the LORD thy God is with thee whithersoever thou goest..." (King James Version, Joshua 1:9).

How many times has fear kept you from doing something: riding a rollercoaster, tobogganing, ice skating, roller skating, starting a new career, dating a new beau, having a gentleman caller, online dating, wearing a new hairstyle, wearing a new dress, trying a new restaurant, going to the movies alone? Fear is the number one thorn that will keep a single woman from enjoying life. Fear is caused by a current condition that has been created by alarm or agitation because of the expectation or realization of danger. We fear because human nature tends to expect the worst or expect danger. When we fear, our mental state becomes one of apprehension or dread. AHHHH, the unknown!

For many of us, the unknown places us within the compounds of fear, sending us full speed ahead to a state of discontentment, and sometimes a life of discontentment. Have you ever met someone who is fearful about anything new? For others it's their everyday life that brings about fear, dread, or apprehension. There is nothing wrong with apprehension, but when apprehension takes over our day-to-day activities, we lose sight of living.

Think about a baby. Isn't it exciting to see how a baby lives life head-on, with no cares in the world? Babies just spend the day smiling, giggling, and playing. They get into mischief because they haven't learned what all the nos that we yell at them mean. They haven't learned all the perimeters that keep them from being afraid of taking chances. Taking steps, moving forward. How often have your recognized fear in the eyes of an infant? Hmmm, never! Because babies do not sense fear. Fear is a learned behavior. Unlike babies, most often we miss out on so many new things because we are fearful.

The Bible gives many examples of those who were fearful of a new assignment when spoken to by the angel of the Lord, until God reassured them and provided comfort through these same words: "Fear Not—Don't be Afraid" (*New Life Application Bible*, 1791).

Abraham
"*After these things the word of the LORD came unto Abram in a vision, saying, Fear not, Abram: I am thy shield, and thy exceeding great reward*" (*King James Version*, Genesis 15:1).

Moses
"*And the LORD said unto Moses, Fear him not: for I have delivered him into thy hand, and all his people, and his land; and thou shalt do to him as thou didst unto Sihon king of the Amorites, which dwelt at Heshbon*" (*King James Version*, Number 21:34).

Joshua
"*And the LORD said unto Joshua, Fear not, neither be thou dismayed: take all the people of war with thee, and arise, go up to Ai: see, I have given into thy hand the king of Ai, and his people, and his city, and his land*" (*King James Version*, Joshua 8:1).

Jeremiah
"*Thou drewest near in the day that I called upon thee: thou saidst, Fear not*" (*King James Version*, Lamentations 3:57).

Daniel
"*Then said he unto me, Fear not, Daniel: for from the first day that thou didst set thine heart to understand and to chasten thyself before thy God, thy words were heard, and I am come for thy words*" (*King James Version*, Daniel 10:12).

Zechariah
"*But the angel said unto him, Fear not, Zacharias: for thy prayer is heard; and thy wife Elisabeth shall bear thee a son, and thou shalt call his name John*" (*King James Version*, Luke 1:13).

Mary
"And the angel said unto her, Fear not, Mary: for thou hast found favour with God" (*King James Version*, Luke 1:30).

Shepherds
"And the angel said unto them, Fear not: for, behold, I bring you good tidings of great joy, which shall be to all people" (*King James Version*, Luke 2:10).

Simon Peter
"And so was also James, and John, the sons of Zebedee, which were partners with Simon. And Jesus said unto Simon, Fear not; from henceforth thou shalt catch men" (*King James Version*, Luke 5:10).

Paul
"For there stood by me this night the angel of God, whose I am, and whom I serve, Saying, Fear not, Paul; thou must be brought before Caesar: and, lo, God hath given thee all them that sail with thee" (*King James Version*, Acts 27:23-24).

John
"And when I saw him, I fell at his feet as dead. And he laid his right hand upon me, saying unto me, Fear not; I am the first and the last: I am he that liveth, and was dead; and, behold, I am alive for evermore, Amen; and have the keys of hell and of death" (*King James Version*, Revelation 1:17-18).

As Christian single women, we must listen for the voice of God and fear not—do not be afraid. If it is of God, then HE will see us through by providing us with everything we need. As long as we are staying in the will of God, we must not fear the unknown. Single women, in order to be content, you must live without constant apprehension.

Thorn of DISCOURAGEMENT

*"When my spirit was overwhelmed within me, then thou knewest my path...
(King James Version, Psalm 142:3)*

*"Behold, the Lord thy God hath set the land before thee: go up and possess
it, as the Lord God of thy fathers hath said unto thee; fear not, neither be
discouraged..." (King James Version, Deuteronomy 1:21).*

There is not a single woman I know that has not experienced
some form of discouragement; there is not a human being I know,
regardless of marital status, that has not experienced discouragement.
Discouragement comes in the form of dating or not dating. Quite
often, we are discouraged because we keep meeting busters, or "non-
potentials," is what I will call them. Discouragement can attack because
we do not have the career we set out to have when we were twenty. As
an undergrad, I majored in Broadcasting Journalism and had this idea
that I would grace everyone's television screen by the time I was 30.
Well, at 30 I was working for Nationwide Insurance and was a full-
time PhD student. There were many days that I became discouraged
because of where I was professionally. I still experience thorns of
discouragement, or that deprivation of confidence, hope, or spirit.

Discouragement is not something that we face alone. Many before
us have also dealt with the thorn of discouragement. Moses and Joshua
both experienced several bouts of discouragement in their mission to
lead the children of Israel. Moses had become so discouraged that
he asked God to kill him. *"And if thou deal thus with me, kill me, I pray
thee, out of hand, if I have found favour in thy sight; and let me not see my
wretchedness..." (King James Version, Numbers 11:15).*

*"And the Lord said unto Joshua, Get thee up; wherefore liest thou thus upon
thy face?" (King James Version, Joshua 7:10).* Joshua was discouraged
when God instructed him to become the successor of Moses and
lead the children of Israel into the land of Canaan. Joshua had been

alongside Moses since childhood and had witnessed first-hand how the Israelites grunted and complained against God. God told them anyone over 20 would not see the promised land, only the new generation of Israelites would (Numbers 32:11).

Constant complaining and constant grumbling makes way for the thorn of discouragement to prick. One has to be careful complaining, not only for themselves, but for those who are listening, because a negative attitude can potentially lead to discouragement for all those listening, including the grumbler and the hearer. Think about it, how often you have overheard or were involved in a conversation in which someone was speaking negatively about a person or situation, which then led to feelings of discouragement because you were personally influenced by the negative nature of the conversation.

An example of a conversation that always begins and ends negatively is the reasons behind why we are single. That conversation always ends in these statements: "I'll never find someone," or, "It's too late," or, "I'm in the wrong city," or, "I let the good one get away," which now has caused an oak tree branch to hang from my side along the seam of my pant leg.

Trials and tribulations can also lead to us becoming discouraged and before we know it, we have lost confidence and hope in a positive outcome. Discouragement causes a drop in our spirit!

The Greek word for discourage is *athumeō*, which means "to be disheartened, dispirited, discouraged," which implies "feeling passion" (Merrill and White, 172). So in other words, when discouragement hits the passion, it becomes negative. Our emotional and behavioral state become negative and downtrodden. We let our hearts become troubled by the negative.

I told you earlier that there is not a human being who has not experienced some level of discouragement. Even the Bible recognizes the men and women who were discouraged as they set out to do the will of the Lord.

Elijah

"But he himself went a day's journey into the wilderness, and came and sat down under a juniper tree: and he requested for himself that he might die; and said, It is enough; now, O Lord, take away my life; for I am not better than my fathers" (King James Version, I Kings 19:4).

Job

"My soul is weary of my life; I will leave my complaint upon myself; I will speak in the bitterness of my soul…" (King James Version, Job 10:1).

David

"O my God, my soul is cast down within me: therefore will I remember thee from the land of Jordan, and of the Hermonites, from the hill Mizar…" (King James Version, Psalm 42:6).

Jeremiah

"Woe is me, my mother, that thou hast borne me a man of strife and a man of contention to the whole earth! I have neither lent on usury, nor men have lent to me on usury; yet every one of them doth curse me…" (King James Version, Jeremiah 15:10).

The Thompson Chain Reference Bible provides ways in which Christians fall prey to discouragement: 1) Hardness of the way; 2) The difficulty of the task; 3) The prosperity of the wicked; and 4) Delay in the fulfillment of desires. These ideas are some of the main causes for seasons of discouragement (Thompson Chain Reference Bible, 1403).

Hardness of the Way

"And they journeyed from mount Hor by the way of the Red sea, to compass the land of Edom: and the soul of the people was much discouraged because of the way…" (King James Version, Numbers 21:4).

Because something is not easy and handed to us with directions, we get discouraged. Living is hard. Life is hard. Not knowing our way can become very frustrating and discouraging. How many times have you become discouraged because the path was not easy to follow? School, career, and family have all presented obstacles in our lives;

how often have we become discouraged because we haven't been able to see light at the end of the tunnel?

The Difficulty of the Task
"And Judah said, The strength of the bearers of burdens is decayed, and there is much rubbish; so that we are not able to build the wall..." (King James Version, Nehemiah 4:10).

You were so excited to begin stacking the numerous books you had stored in boxes on your new bookshelf. Seeing the picture of the bookshelf was nothing in comparison to the directions for assembly. Instead of just taking your time and working your way through the assembly of the bookshelf, you immediately began to rant and rave. Ahhh, stop for a second, relax; your mind is going to a negative place, a place of discouragement and frustration. The road is not always easy, but God did not bring you this far to leave you.

The Prosperity of the Wicked
"But as for me, my feet were almost gone; my steps had well-nigh slipped. For I was envious at the foolish, when I saw the prosperity of the wicked..." (King James Version, Psalm 73:2-3).

"That was supposed to be my _____ ! That should have been me! I don't understand why they have it and I don't. Why did they get the job and I didn't?" In your minute eyesight, the wicked are prospering while you are slowly acquiring nothing. Not true, my sister. The wicked are prospering from your perception, not the perception of God. The old familiar saying, all that glitters is not gold, could not be more true when we compare/contrast our situations based on the situations of others. Stop letting another's prosperity get you down; define and achieve your own prosperity according to your obedience to the word of God.

Delay in Fulfillment of Desires

"Hope deferred maketh the heart sick: but when the desire cometh, it is a tree of life..." (King James Version, Proverbs 13:12).

How long must I wait, Lord? I have been waiting forever! I always use to hear my dad say, "When is my ship going to come in?" I think he died waiting on that ship. God's delay is not our denial. In order for our desires to be fulfilled, they must align with God's will.

In the book of Ruth, Ruth and Naomi definitely had reason to be discouraged, with the death of Naomi's two sons and the death of a husband for Ruth; why wouldn't these women be discouraged? Discouragement causes the single woman to lose hope! At all cost we must try and avoid discouragement. Christians do not have to lose hope, because we have constant hope in Jesus Christ! The thorn of discouragement can cause us to focus on the non-optimistic side of things—the glass being half-empty instead of half-full. Who cares whether the glass is half-full or half-empty? Our focus should be on the One who fills the glass full.

Thorn of LONELINESS

"And he that sent me is with me: the Father hath not left me alone; for I do always those things that please him" (King James Version, John 8:29).

As Christian women, we are never alone because we have been surrounded, embraced, and covered in God's love. However, there does exist what I call a thorn or state of loneliness that comes about when we don't feel the human presence of others. To be lonely means that you are without companions, characterized by aloneness, solitary, unfrequented by people, desolate. Thorns of loneliness can even occur when you are surrounded by people, because internally there is a yearning or a longing for something. The difference between a thorn of loneliness and being alone is the presence of God. Christian women, we have a surety in God and his presence, for he promised that he *"will not leave thee nor forsake thee…"* (*King James Version*, Hebrews 13:5). This particular verse gives us concrete evidence that God will never leave us and with God, we are never alone. For in this verse no matter how you read it, whether it's read forward or backward, it still confirms that God will never leave us.

I will not leave thee nor forsake thee.
Thee forsake nor thee fail not will I.

God has provided us with a Comforter in the Holy Spirit, who continually resides in us to help us through in our current state of singleness. *"And I will pray the Father, and he shall give you another **Comforter**, that he may abide with you forever"* (*King James Version*, John 14:16).

The great thing about the word of God is that it gives us clear examples of others—Jacob, Joseph, Elijah, Jeremiah, Nehemiah, Christ, and Paul—who also have experienced the same thorns that we encounter in our daily lives (Guidepost Family Concordance, 421).

Jacob experienced loneliness in prayer
"And he took them, and sent them over the brook, and sent over that he had. And Jacob was left alone; and there wrestled a man with him until the breaking of the day. And when he saw that he prevailed not against him, he touched the hollow of his thigh; and the hollow of Jacob's thigh was out of joint, as he wrestled with him. And he said, Let me go, for the day breaketh. And he said, I will not let thee go, except thou bless me. And he said unto him, What is thy name? And he said, Jacob. And he said, Thy name shall be called no more Jacob, but Israel: for as a prince hast thou power with God and with men, and hast prevailed. And Jacob asked him, and said, Tell me, I pray thee, thy name. And he said, Wherefore is it that thou dost ask after my name? And he blessed him there. And Jacob called the name of the place Peniel: for I have seen God face to face, and my life is preserved" (*King James Version*, Genesis 32:23-30).

28

Joseph experienced loneliness in weeping

"And Joseph made haste; for his bowels did yearn upon his brother: and he sought where to weep; and he entered into his chamber, and wept there. And he washed his face, and went out, and refrained himself, and said, Set on bread" *(King James Version*, Genesis 43:30-31).

Elijah experienced loneliness in Discouragement

"And when he saw that, he arose, and went for his life, and came to Beersheba, which belongeth to Judah, and left his servant there. But he himself went a day's journey into the wilderness and came and sat down under a juniper tree: and he requested for himself that he might die; and said, It is enough; now, O Lord, take away my life; for I am not better than my fathers. And as he lay and slept under a juniper tree, behold, then an angel touched him, and said unto him, Arise and eat. And he looked, and, behold, there was a cake baken on the coals, and a cruse of water at his head. And he did eat and drink, and laid him down again. And the angel of the Lord came again the second time, and touched him, and said, Arise and eat; because the journey is too great for thee. And he arose, and did eat and drink, and went in the strength of that meat forty days and forty nights unto Horeb the mount of God. And he came thither unto a cave, and lodged there; and, behold, the word of the Lord came to him, and he said unto him, What doest thou here, Elijah? And he said, I have been very jealous for the Lord God of hosts: for the children of Israel have forsaken thy covenant, thrown down thine altars, and slain thy prophets with the sword; and I, even I only, am left; and they seek my life, to take it away. And he said, Go forth, and stand upon the mount before the Lord. And, behold, the Lord passed by, and a great and strong wind rent the mountains, and brake in pieces the rocks before the Lord; but the Lord was not in the wind: and after the wind an earthquake; but the Lord was not in the earthquake: And after the earthquake a fire; but the Lord was not in the fire: and after the fire a still small voice. And it was so, when Elijah heard it, that he wrapped his face in his mantle, and went out, and stood in the entering in of the cave. And, behold, there came a voice unto him, and said, What doest thou here, Elijah? And he said, I have been very jealous for the Lord God of hosts: because the children of Israel have forsaken thy covenant, thrown down thine altars, and slain thy prophets with the sword; and I, even I only, am left; and they seek my life, to take it away" *(King James Version*, I Kings 19:3-14).

Jeremiah experienced loneliness in witnessing

"I sat not in the assembly of the mockers, nor rejoiced; I sat alone because of thy hand: for thou hast filled me with indignation" (King James Version, Jeremiah 15:17).

Nehemiah experienced loneliness in a night vigil

"And I arose in the night, I and some few men with me; neither told I any man what my God had put in my heart to do at Jerusalem: neither was there any beast with me, save the beast that I rode upon. And I went out by night by the gate of the valley, even before the dragon well, and to the dung port, and viewed the walls of Jerusalem, which were broken down, and the gates thereof were consumed with fire. Then I went on to the gate of the fountain, and to the king's pool: but there was no place for the beast that was under me to pass. Then went I up in the night by the brook, and viewed the wall, and turned back, and entered by the gate of the valley, and so returned. And the rulers knew not whither I went, or what I did; neither had I as yet told it to the Jews, nor to the priests, nor to the nobles, nor to the rulers, nor to the rest that did the work" (King James Version, Nehemiah 2:12-16).

Christ experienced loneliness in agony

"Then cometh Jesus with them unto a place called Gethsemane, and saith unto the disciples. Sit ye here, while I go and pray yonder. And he took with him Peter and the two sons of Zebedee, and began to be sorrowful and very heavy. Then saith he unto them, My soul is exceeding sorrowful, even unto death: tarry ye here, and watch with me. And he went a little farther, and fell on his face, and prayed, saying, O my Father, if it be possible, let this cup pass from me: nevertheless, not as I will, but as thou wilt. And he cometh unto the disciples, and findeth them asleep, and saith unto Peter, What, could ye not watch with me one hour? Watch and pray, that ye enter not into temptation: the spirit indeed is willing, but the flesh is weak. He went away again the second time, and prayed, saying, O my Father, if this cup may not pass away from me, except I drink it, thy will be done. And he came and found them asleep again: for their eyes were heavy. And he left them, and went away again, and prayed the third time, saying the same words. Then cometh he to his disciples, and saith unto them, Sleep on now, and take your rest: behold, the hour is at hand, and the Son of man is betrayed into the hands of sinners" (King James Version, Matthew 26:36-45).

<u>Paul experienced loneliness in prison</u>
"At my first answer, no man stood with me, but all men forsook me: I pray God that it may not be laid to their charge" (King James Version, 2 Timothy 4:16).

The assurance that we have in Christ Jesus as single Christian women is that although we may feel lonely, we are never alone, as the words in the hymn "Never Alone" promise.

> *No, never alone, no never alone,*
> *He promised never to leave me,*
> *He'll claim me for His own;*
> *No, never alone, no never alone.*
> *He promised never to leave me,*
> *Never to leave me alone.*

Thorn of DOUBT

> *"And immediately Jesus stretched forth his hand, and caught him, and said unto him, O thou of little faith, wherefore didst thou doubt?" (King James Version,* Matthew 14:31).

Doubt is not a new concept. The word *doubt* is used 13 times in the Bible. *Doubted,* 4 times; *doubteth,* 1 time; *doubtful,* 2 times; *doubting,* 4 times; *doubtless,* 7 times; and *doubts,* 2 times. Doubt is the uncertainty of mind, to be undecided or skeptical about something, to tend to disbelieve, distrust, to suspect, fear. *Aporeō,* the Greek word for doubt, means "to be without a way . . . to be without resources, embarrassed, in doubt, perplexity, at a loss" (Vine, Unger and White, eds., 182).

The disciples doubted of who would betray Jesus and the absence of his body from the tomb. *"Then the disciples looked one on another, doubting of whom he spake" (King James Version,* John 13:22). Festus was in doubt about the nature of the accusations brought against Paul. *"And because I doubted of such manner of questions, I asked him whether he would go to Jerusalem, and there be judged of these matters" (King James Version,* Acts

25:20). *"Being at a loss how to investigate these questions, I asked whether he wished to go to Jerusalem and be tried there regarding them"* (*Revised Standard Version*, Acts 25:20). *"I desire to be present with you now, and to change my Voice; for I stand in doubt of you"* (*King James Version*, Galatians 4:20). "I could wish to be present with you now and to change my tone, for I am perplexed about you" (*Revised Standard Version*, Galatians 4:20; Vine, Unger, and White, 182).

Doubt is something that is not new to the Bible, both in the Old and New Testament. Sarah and Abraham both doubted God in the Old Testament in the conception of their son Isaac. Moses doubted when God told him to return to Egypt to lead the children of Israel, the Israelites, when they faced difficulties in the desert. Gideon, when he would be a judge and a leader. Zechariah, when God told him he would be a father in his old age. And Thomas doubted the resurrection of Jesus Christ (*New Life Application Bible*, 1789).

Abraham—When God told him he would be a father in old age
"And God said unto Abraham, As for Sarai thy wife, thou shalt not call her name Sarai, but Sarah shall her name be. And I will bless her, and give thee a son also of her: yea, I will bless her, and she shall be a mother of nations; kings of people shall be of her. Then Abraham fell upon his face, and laughed, and said in his heart, Shall a child be born unto him that is an hundred years old? and shall Sarah, that is ninety years old, bear? And Abraham said unto God, O that Ishmael might live before thee! And God said, Sarah thy wife shall bear thee a son indeed; and thou shalt call his name Isaac: and I will establish my covenant with him for an everlasting covenant, and with his seed after him" (*King James Version*, Genesis 17:15-19).

Sarah—When God told her she would be a mother in old age
"And they said unto him, Where is Sarah thy wife? And he said, Behold, in the tent. And he said, I will certainly return unto thee according to the time of life; and, lo, Sarah thy wife shall have a son. And Sarah heard it in the tent door, which was behind him. Now Abraham and Sarah were old and well stricken in age; and it ceased to be with Sarah after the manner of women. Therefore Sarah laughed within herself, saying, After I am waxed old shall I have pleasure, my lord being old also? And the LORD said unto Abraham, Wherefore did Sarah

laugh, saying, Shall I of a surety bear a child, which am old? Is anything too hard for the LORD? At the time appointed I will return unto thee, according to the time of life, and Sarah shall have a son. Then Sarah denied, saying, I laughed not; for she was afraid. And he said, Nay; but thou didst laugh" (King James Version, Genesis 18:9-15).

Moses—When God told him to return to Egypt to lead the children of Israel

"Come now therefore, and I will send thee unto Pharaoh, that thou mayest bring forth my people the children of Israel out of Egypt. And Moses said unto God, Who am I, that I should go unto Pharaoh, and that I should bring forth the children of Israel out of Egypt? And he said, Certainly I will be with thee; and this shall be a token unto thee, that I have sent thee: When thou hast brought forth the people out of Egypt, ye shall serve God upon this mountain. And Moses said unto God, Behold, when I come unto the children of Israel, and shall say unto them, The God of your fathers hath sent me unto you; and they shall say to me, What is his name? what shall I say unto them? And God said unto Moses, I AM THAT I AM: and he said, Thus shalt thou say unto the children of Israel, I AM hath sent me unto you. And God said moreover unto Moses, Thus shalt thou say unto the children of Israel, the LORD God of your fathers, the God of Abraham, the God of Isaac, and the God of Jacob, hath sent me unto you: this is my name for ever, and this is my memorial unto all generations" (King James Version, Exodus 3:10-15).

Israelites—Whenever they faced difficulties in the desert

"And they took their journey from Elim, and all the congregation of the children of Israel came unto the wilderness of Sin, which is between Elim and Sinai, on the fifteenth day of the second month after their departing out of the land of Egypt. And the whole congregation of the children of Israel murmured against Moses and Aaron in the wilderness: And the children of Israel said unto them, Would to God we had died by the hand of the LORD in the land of Egypt, when we sat by the flesh pots, and when we did eat bread to the full; for ye have brought us forth into this wilderness, to kill this whole assembly with hunger" (King James Version, Exodus 16:1-3).

Gideon—When told he would be a judge and leader

"And the LORD looked upon him, and said, Go in this thy might, and thou shalt save Israel from the hand of the Midianites: have not I sent thee? And he said unto him, Oh my Lord, wherewith shall I save Israel? behold, my family is poor

in Manasseh, and I am the least in my father's house. And the LORD said unto him, Surely I will be with thee, and thou shalt smite the Midianites as one man. And he said unto him, If now I have found grace in thy sight, then shew me a sign that thou talkest with me. Depart not hence, I pray thee, until I come unto thee, and bring forth my present, and set it before thee. And he said, I will tarry until thou come again. And Gideon went in, and made ready a kid, and unleavened cakes of an ephah of flour: the flesh he put in a basket, and he put the broth in a pot, and brought it out unto him under the oak, and presented it. And the angel of God said unto him, Take the flesh and the unleavened cakes, and lay them upon this rock, and pour out the broth. And he did so. Then the angel of the LORD put forth the end of the staff that was in his hand, and touched the flesh and the unleavened cakes; and there rose up fire out of the rock, and consumed the flesh and the unleavened cakes. Then the angel of the LORD departed out of his sight. And when Gideon perceived that he was an angel of the LORD, Gideon said, Alas, O LORD God! for because I have seen an angel of the LORD face to face. And the LORD said unto him, Peace be unto thee; fear not: thou shalt not die" (King James Version, Judges 6:14-23).

Zechariah—When God told him he would be a father in old age
"And Zacharias said unto the angel, Whereby shall I know this? for I am an old man, and my wife well stricken in years" (King James Version, Luke 1:18).

Thomas –When he was told Jesus had risen from the dead
"But Thomas, one of the twelve, called Didymus, was not with them when Jesus came. The other disciples therefore said unto him, We have seen the LORD. But he said unto them, Except I shall see in his hands the print of the nails, and put my finger into the print of the nails, and thrust my hand into his side, I will not believe" (King James Version, John 20:24-25).

Doubt is not unusual. Notice how God used doubters to accomplish great things. As believers, we have to remember that none of the thorns we experience are necessarily bad things unless they begin to cause us to lose our peace and joy. They become bad when we let them overtake who we are in Christ Jesus. The flesh will cause us not to see the power of Jesus Christ, the awesomeness of what he can do. Historically, Christians doubted Christ in four forms. Doubt in Christ's miracles (Matthew 12:24-30). Doubt in the resurrection of

Christ (John 20:24-20). Doubt in Christ being the Messiah (Luke 7:9-20). And doubt in the return of Christ. *"And saying, Where is the promise of his coming? for since the fathers fell asleep, all things continue as they were from the beginning of the creation"* (King James Version, 2 Peter 3:4; Guidepost Family Concordance, 194).

If they doubted Christ when he was visibly present, why wouldn't we as believers doubt Christ in the spirit? It is so easy to get caught up in the thorn of doubt. Satan has so many tactics to trick us into doubt for a state of discontentment. Why should God do that for you? Have you really been obedient? Do you deserve it? Does he have the power to do that? Satan is the mastermind of trickery. *"The thief cometh not, but for to steal, and to kill, and to destroy: I am come that they might have life, and that they might have it more abundantly"* (King James Version, John 10:10). But the shouting part is that Jesus Christ has come to give us life abundantly!

__Thorn of CONFUSION__

"For God is not the author of confusion, but of peace, as in all churches of the saints" (King James Version, I Corinthians 1:33).

There are so many times as single women we get involved in states of confusion. I think the most often is in dating and friendships. *Confusion* is "to be perplexed or throw off. To assemble without order or sense. To make unclear; blur" (Webster's Dictionary, 237). God is not a God of confusion. He does not operate in confusion, but many of us live our lives in confusion. We constantly find ourselves in situations of confusion. Whether in relationships, dating, and/or work, we engage in a state of always being thrown off-kilter. Confusion is another form of distraction, to get and keep your mind off of the good things of life.

Herod was perplexed about John the Baptist. *"For Herod feared John, knowing that he was a righteous and holy man, and kept Him safe (Revised Standard Version, Mark 6:20).* The disciples were confused. *"And it came to pass, as they were much perplexed thereabout, behold, two men stood by them in shining garments"* (*King James Version*, Luke 24:4). Paul was perplexed in his trial experiences. *"We are troubled on every side, yet not distressed; we are perplexed, but not in despair"* (*King James Version*, 2 Corinthians 4:8; Anderson, 100).

Akatastasia, "instability," denotes "a state of disorder, disturbance, confusion, tumult or commotions." But God lets believers know that he is not a God of confusion (Vine, Unger, and White, 122).

The Bible outlines five causes of confusion: the tongue, fleshly characteristics, people, enemies, and God's will.

<u>The Tongue</u>
"And the tongue is a fire, a world of iniquity: so is the tongue among our members, that it defileth the whole body, and setteth on fire the course of nature; and it is set on fire of hell" (*King James Version*, James 3:6).

<u>Fleshly Characteristics</u>
"For I fear, lest, when I come, I shall not find you such as I would, and that I shall be found unto you such as ye would not: lest there be debates, envyings, wraths, strifes, backbitings, whisperings, swellings, tumults" (*King James Version*, 2 Corinthian 1:20).

"For where envying and strife is, there is confusion and every evil work" (*King James Version*, James 3:16).

<u>People</u>
"And the whole city was filled with confusion: and having caught Gaius and Aristarchus, men of Macedonia, Paul's companions in travel, they rushed with one accord into the theatre" (*King James Version*, Act 19:29).

"Some therefore cried one thing, and some another: for the assembly was confused: and the more part knew not wherefore they were come together; to be in confusion" (*King James Version*, Acts 19:32).

And as they went about to kill him, tidings came unto the chief captain of the band, that all Jerusalem was in an uproar" (King James Version, Acts 21:31).

Enemies

"Let them be ashamed and confounded that seek after my soul: let them be turned backward, and put to confusion, that desire my hurt" (King James Version, Psalm 70:2).

God's will

"Then came David to Nob to Ahimelech the priest: and Ahimelech was afraid at the meeting of David, and said unto him, Why art thou alone, and no man with thee? And David said unto Ahimelech the priest, The king hath commanded me a business, and hath said unto me, Let no man know anything of the business whereabout I send thee, and what I have commanded thee: and I have appointed my servants to such and such a place. Now therefore what is under thine hand? give me five loaves of bread in mine hand, or what there is present. And the priest answered David, and said, There is no common bread undermine hand, but there is hallowed bread; if the young men have kept themselves at least from women. And David answered the priest, and said unto him, Of a truth women have been kept from us about these three days, since I came out, and the vessels of the young men are holy, and the bread is in a manner common, yea, though it were sanctified this day in the vessel. So the priest gave him hallowed bread: for there was no bread there but the shewbread, that was taken from before the LORD, *to put hot bread in the day when it was taken away. Now a certain man of the servants of Saul was there that day, detained before the* LORD; *and his name was Doeg, an Edomite, the chiefest of the herdmen that belonged to Saul. And David said unto Ahimelech, And is there not here under thine hand spear or sword? for I have neither brought my sword nor my weapons with me, because the king's business required haste. And the priest said, The sword of Goliath the Philistine, whom thou slewest in the valley of Elah, behold, it is here wrapped in a cloth behind the ephod: if thou wilt take that, take it: for there is no other save that here. And David said, There is none like that; give it me. And David arose and fled that day for fear of Saul, and went to Achish the king of Gath. And the servants of Achish said unto him, Is not this David the king of the land? did they not sing one to another of him in dances, saying, Saul hath slain his thousands, and David his ten thousands? And David laid up these words in his heart, and was sore afraid of Achish the king of Gath" (King James Version,* I Samuel 23:1-12).

The tongue, flesh, people, and God's will are sources of confusion. When we speak, we must be careful of the things that flow from our tongue, because the wrong words can create a whirlwind of confusion. People and the flesh can also be causes of confusion. God's will is never a source of confusion. The confusion comes when we are disobedient to HIS will and/or we ignore HIS voice then we create the confusion for ourselves. Confusion creates discomfort.

Thorn of DEPRESSION

"A merry heart doeth good like a medicine: but a broken spirit drieth the bones..." (King James Version, Proverbs 17:22).

I've known many single friends who have spent countless hours in their beds or on their couches instead of living life. It is so easy for us to find ourselves in states of depression because things aren't what we think they should be; and the operative words are "what we think they should be." I think that is how we find ourselves so often in states of depression, because we have outlined what we think our lives should be instead of living our lives in obedience to God and his will for our lives. He didn't call, he calls too much, and he doesn't call enough. He didn't ask me out. I have nothing to wear. I'm tired. I'm hungry. The excuses we place on our lives lead us to depression.

Over the past few years, I've run into men who suffer from bouts of depression. I remember a guy that someone was trying to get me to date. I talked to him a few times and then didn't hear from him for a while (and yes, I was in my state of stubbornness—that's another book). However, when I finally heard from him, he revealed to me that he had been depressed and in bed for weeks. Now quite honestly it scared me, because in my mind I did the stereotypical thing. "If a man can't handle his emotions or problems, then he can't handle me." But that was far from the truth of what depression is. It wasn't that he could not handle his emotions or problems. It was that he let the problem get the best of his current state. Depression affects us all. It is brought on when our conditions lead us to being down or our spirit becomes low and ultimately we find ourselves in a state of depression. Depression is a heavy weight; it is a state of feeling sad or melancholy. Serious bouts of depression can lead to a psychotic or neurotic condition characterized by an inability to concentrate, insomnia, and feelings of gloominess and guilt.

The word of God does not give a direct indication of individuals who suffered from depression, but there are many examples of those who could have taken on a state of depression because of their circumstance.

Hannah's longing for a child

"But unto Hannah he gave a worthy portion; for he loved Hannah: but the LORD had shut up her womb. And her adversary also provoked her sore, for to make her fret, because the LORD had shut up her womb. And as he did so year by year, when she went up to the house of the LORD, so she provoked her; therefore she wept, and did not eat. Then said Elkanah her husband to her, Hannah, why weepest thou? and why eatest thou not? and why is thy heart grieved? am not I better to thee than ten sons? So Hannah rose up after they had eaten in Shiloh, and after they had drunk. Now Eli the priest sat upon a seat by a post of the temple of the LORD. And she was in bitterness of soul, and prayed unto the LORD, and wept sore. And she vowed a vow, and said, O LORD of hosts, if thou wilt indeed look on the affliction of thine handmaid, and remember me, and not forget thine handmaid, but wilt give unto thine handmaid a man child, then I will give him unto the LORD all the days of his life, and there shall no razor come upon his head. And it came to pass, as she continued praying before the LORD, that Eli marked her mouth. Now Hannah, she spake in her heart; only her lips moved, but her voice was not heard: therefore Eli thought she had been drunken. And Eli said unto her, How long wilt thou be drunken? put away thy wine from thee. And Hannah answered and said, No, my lord, I am a woman of a sorrowful spirit: I have drunk neither wine nor strong drink, but have poured out my soul before the LORD" (King James Version, I Samuel 1:4-6).

DR. HEATHER E. BURTON

David's coveting of another's wife

"And it came to pass, after the year was expired, at the time when kings go forth to battle, that David sent Joab, and his servants with him, and all Israel; and they destroyed the children of Ammon, and besieged Rabbah. But David tarried still at Jerusalem. And it came to pass in an eveningtide, that David arose from off his bed, and walked upon the roof of the king's house: and from the roof he saw a woman washing herself; and the woman was very beautiful to look upon. And David sent and enquired after the woman. And one said, Is not this Bathsheba, the daughter of Eliam, the wife of Uriah the Hittite? And David sent messengers, and took her; and she came in unto him, and he lay with her; for she was purified from her uncleanness: and she returned unto her house" (King James Version, 2 Samuel 11:2-4).

Job in the loss of all his possessions

"And where is now my hope? as for my hope, who shall see it?" (King James Version, Job 17:15).

Mary and Martha's loss of their brother and the absence of Jesus

"Then Martha, as soon as she heard that Jesus was coming, went and met him: but Mary sat still in the house. Then said Martha unto Jesus, Lord, if thou hadst been here, my brother had not died" (King James Version, John 6:20-21).

Job losses, wanting children, wanting a husband, wanting someone else's husband, can lead us to states of depression. Because again we become so focused on what we don't have that it takes over every thought that we do, leading us to sad music, tear-jerker television shows, and long night pillow cries. Depression sucks the hope out of a Christian. As Christians, we should not be like the dead (emotionless) because we have hope in Jesus Christ. *"But I would not have you to be ignorant, brethren, concerning them which are asleep, that ye sorrow not, even as others which have no hope"* (King James Version, I Thessalonians 4:1).

Thorn of ANXIETY

"Let your moderation be known unto all men. The Lord is at hand. Be careful for nothing; but in everything by prayer

40

*and supplication with thanksgiving let your requests be made
known unto God. And the peace of God, which passeth all
understanding, shall keep your hearts and minds through
Christ Jesus" (King James Version,* Philippians 4:5-7).

How many times have you heard, "I think too much"? Is there a
difference between thinking too much and worry? When we take a
thought or concentrate on something too long it becomes a possession
of our minds, our focus. Single women often focus too much on their
state of being single instead of living as a single woman. We get caught
up in the thoughts of being single, which then creates worriedness
about being single. But the word of God tells us why worry about
tomorrow or take thought for our life.

<u>Take no thought</u>
*"Therefore I say unto you, Take no thought for your life, what ye shall eat, or
what ye shall drink; nor yet for your body, what ye shall put on. Is not the life
more than meat, and the body than raiment? Behold the fowls of the air: for they
sow not, neither do they reap, nor gather into barns; yet your heavenly Father
feedeth them. Are ye not much better than they? Which of you by taking thought
can add one cubit unto his stature?" (King James Version,* Matthew 6:25-27).

Worry or anxiety, anxiousness, care, concern, solicitude, are all
words to define a thorn that separates us from a state of peacefulness
with God. Anxiety is a state of uneasiness and distress about future
uncertainties; apprehension; worry. A thorn of anxiousness means that
we have become worried, stressed, and uneasy about some uncertain
event or matter.

<u>Hagar was anxious about the future of her son</u>
*"And she went, and sat her down over against him a good way off, as it were a bow
shot: for she said, Let me not see the death of the child. And she sat over against
him, and lift up her voice, and wept. And God heard the voice of the lad; and the
angel of God called to Hagar out of heaven, and said unto her, What aileth thee,
Hagar? fear not; for God hath heard the voice of the lad where he is. Arise, lift up
the lad, and hold him in thine hand; for I will make him a great nation. And God*

opened her eyes, and she saw a well of water; and she went, and filled the bottle with water, and gave the lad drink" (King James Version, Genesis 21:16-19).

God tells us to cast our burdens and cares on him.

--GOD CAN HANDLE ALL OUR THORNS--

"Humble yourselves therefore under the mighty hand of God, that he may exalt you in due time: Casting all your cares upon him; for he careth for you. Be sober, be vigilant; because your adversary the devil, as a roaring lion, walketh about, seeking whom he may devour: Whom resist stedfast in the faith, knowing that the same afflictions are accomplished in your brethren that are in the world. But the God of all grace, who hath called us unto his eternal glory by Christ Jesus, after that ye have suffered a while, make you perfect, stablish, strengthen, settle you. To him be glory and dominion for ever and ever. Amen" (King James Version, I Peter 5:7-11).

CHAPTER FOUR

UNDERSTANDING YOUR PERSONAL THORNS & WHERE THEY LEAD

No matter how we dress it up, change it, reword it, or look at it differently, thorns lead to states of discontentment. Thorns cause us to become emotionally, mentally, and behaviorally disconnected from the will of God because we become focused on the problem instead of the Problem Solver. Since there are so many situations that can lead us to having thorns in our lives and states of discontentment, we must be able to recognize how thorns personally and individually affect us.

In the last chapter, I discussed different thorns that lead to discontentment. In looking at these thorns, it's imperative that we recognize how one or two thorns can join together and form an entanglement of weeds in our lives to keep us discontent or distracted from enjoying being single. It is easy for us to get entrapped in one area of discontentment, which then causes other states of discontentment to form. For instance, a thorn of fear can also lead us to a thorn of loneliness. We get so caught up in fearing the unknown that we never associate ourselves with others or new situations. In order to be content in our current states of singleness, we must learn to identify what thorns personally cause discontentment in our lives. Once we are able to identify the thorns that prick and prod at our sides, creating discontentment, we can learn to stop feeding the thorns into fully cultivated bushes.

Understanding your personal thorns allows for contentment in that it keeps you focused on what you have, and not on what you have not. Just as the children of Israel complained about not having meat to eat in Numbers 11:6, we have to learn to appreciate what we have instead of what we do not have. "We should not allow our unfulfilled desires to cause us to forget God's gift of life, food, health, work and friends" (*Life Application Bible*, 232). I may not have a husband, but I do have God!

"Therefore the place was named Ki broth Hattaavah because there they buried the people who had craved other food" (*New Life Application Bible*, Numbers 11:34). The New Life Application Bible puts it this way: "Craving or lusting is more than inappropriate sexual desire. It can be an unnatural or greedy desire for anything (sports, knowledge, possessions, and influence over others). In this circumstance, God punished the Israelites for craving good food! Their desire was not wrong; the sin was in allowing that desire to turn into greed. They felt it was their right to have fine food, and they could think of nothing else. When you become preoccupied with something until it affects your perspective on everything else, you have moved from desire to lust" (*Life Application Bible*, 233).

Is FEAR Your THORN?

Our deepest fear is not that we are inadequate. Our deepest fear is that we are powerful beyond measure. It is our light, not our darkness that most frightens us. We ask ourselves, 'Who am I to be brilliant, gorgeous, talented, fabulous?' Actually, who are you not to be? You are a child of God. Playing small does not serve the world. There is nothing enlightened about shrinking so that other people won't feel insecure around you. We are all meant to shine,

as children do. We were born to make manifest the glory of God that is within us. It's not just in some of us; it's in everyone. And as we let our own light shine, we unconsciously give other people permission to do the same. As we are liberated from our own fear, our presence automatically liberates others.
— Marianne Williamson, *A Return to Love: Reflections on the Principles of "A Course in Miracles"*

Franklin D. Roosevelt said that "The only thing we have to fear is, fear itself." Fear itself has kept me from progressing at a quicker pace than had I not feared outcomes. Think about it. Throughout life, how often have you gotten caught in the art of fearing? And what we fear is the outcome itself. If we learn to stop fearing fear, then we begin to take action at a more rapid pace instead of contemplating the outcomes. We begin to take steps to overtake the situations that cause us to be fearful.

I remember receiving a text message from a guy I had been dating for a few months. Immediately after reading the text message, I began to fear the outcome instead of taking things in context for what it was worth for the moment. The text message was about a job—and from that, a sense of immediate apprehension overtook me and my mind began to wander to the only two scenarios that could come from this job; either we would not go any further than where we were now, or I'd have to uproot my whole life because it would progress into a permanent commitment. I swear I broke out in a sweat over these two outcomes. Who wants to be disappointed again because a relationship doesn't work? Or who wants to uproot their whole life? Hey, I got it pretty good right now, and right here.

But before I let the thorns of fear take me into a state of discontentment, I stopped and said, "Lord, thank you for what I have right now. Help me to live in this moment and let your will guide the rest." Instantaneously, a sense of peace came over me…that peace that passeth all understanding because I don't know what the future holds but I can't let fear of the future dictate my present state of contentment.

Fear has even caused me to miss out on some fun times by getting caught in the fear of "What if someone sees me with him?" If I really did not like a guy I would not go out with him because I "feared" that someone would see me with him. All of these thoughts would run rapidly through my mind. Will that ruin my chances with the next one or the one I really like? I don't want anyone to see me with him, he's lame, and he's a buster. He's going to ruin my image. Can't have that! I can still hear my girl's voice ringing in my head, "It is only a date! Why are you so concerned about who sees you?" It was the fear factor. I was in a state of fear. And I label this as a state of fear because this thought pattern dictated and limited my dating experience. Instead of going to the Cavs game, the Browns game, dinner, the movies, concerts—I opted out because I did not want to be seen with this one (and I say that in respect to more than one guy).

I use this analogy because the fear of me being seen with someone kept me in a state; a condition. I was afraid of being caught. I had apprehension about who I may run into, instead of just going and living life. Today I am no longer in this particular state of fear, but I do have boundaries as to who I say yes to. Because trust me when I say, I have been approached by some real doozies.

Fear causes us to miss out on the blessings God has for us because it causes us to not want to step out on faith. When we fear, we begin to allow the enemy to confuse his attacks with the voice of God. We must remove fear from our being in order to hear the voice of God and live life to the fullest in accordance with God's will. The will of God will never lead us in the wrong direction; but fearing that God does not have our best interest at heart will lead us to an unfulfilled life.

What creates fear in your life? What causes you to become overwhelmed by the thorn of fear? It's important to pinpoint what idiosyncrasies cause apprehension in your life. Is it the fear of being hurt? Is it the fear of being alone? Is it the fear of saying something wrong? Is it the fear of failing? Is it the fear of dying alone? What causes fear in your life? Take a few minutes and begin to identify your fear factors. Think about what makes you break out into a sweat. What makes your heart beat 10 times faster? What causes you to have to take deep breaths? Maybe it's public speaking, maybe it's singing. Maybe you are worried about what other people will think. Overcome fear by facing fear head-on.

Fear is nothing more than a result of self-doubt, and self-doubt is an attack of the enemy. Satan uses weapons of self-doubt to make us apprehend the worst possible outcomes. When you feel the thorn overtaking you—STOP the apprehension before it starts! PRAY. Lord, help me to have peace beyond my own understanding! BREATHE Deep breaths as you pray! And reflect on *"Fear thou not; for I am with thee: be not dismayed; for I am thy God: I will strengthen thee; yea, I will help thee; yea, I will uphold thee with the right hand of my righteousness" (King James Version*, Isaiah 41:10).

> *I have learned over the years that when one's mind is made up, this diminishes fear; knowing what must be done does away with fear.*
> *~Rosa Parks*

Is DISCOURAGEMENT Your THORN?

> *The Christian life is not a constant high. I have my moments of deep discouragement. I have to go to God in prayer with tears in my eyes, and say, "O God, forgive me," or "Help me."*
> *~Billy Graham*

Discouragement, discouragement, discouragement—why wouldn't I be discouraged? You may ask. I ask, why should you be discouraged? And of course I hear you saying, "I am discouraged because I keep dating only to still be single, while all my friends are married. I am discouraged because my children are not headed in a direction I would like them to be. I am discouraged because my husband cheated and left me for another woman." The thorn of discouragement is not unusual. I have been discouraged over and over again in the world of dating. I have been disappointed by this one, let down by that one, and pissed off by him over there. After so many letdowns, who wouldn't be discouraged? The thorn of discouragement becomes a problem when it places you in a state of discontentment because discouragement causes you to focus too much on what you don't have or what you have not achieved.

I can remember during the last stages of writing my dissertation being unemployed and headed for graduation. The last two years of my program I spent working in a fellowship position, and long story short, I was promised full-time employment after graduation by my direct supervisor, but when she was not rehired, the director of the agency told me he did not promise me that position and my contract would end that current year. Now needless to say, the director eventually lost his job and was replaced because of his unfair practices and "God don't like ugly"—that's all I will say about that. The ending of this contract left me in pursuit of new employment.

As I began to look for employment, I started receiving rejection after rejection because here I was about to obtain a PhD and had little experience in that particular field; at least not enough to obtain more than an entry or mid-level position. For months I was told that I had too much education and not enough experience, or something that hurt my feelings, or the salary was minimal. And of course I thought after such a high achievement, there was no way I was going to accept a minimal salary.

Ironically, I did except a minimal salary; the same salary an employer offered me in February was what I accepted in October. After months of unemployment my mindset changed and I had to get out of the state of discouragement that was holding me back. Was I discouraged that my salary was so low to have a PhD? Of course. But

I used this opportunity to prove I had the ability and skills to move into a higher position, and today I am in a higher-paying and higher-ranking position. If I had let the thorn of discouragement halt me from continuing to apply for jobs, I would have ended in a severe state of discontentment because of the financial stress and burdens of life that would have been upon me. And during this bout of unemployment, not once was I late on a bill. Not once did my credit score drop, and not once did I not make a 30-minute meal after watching Rachel Ray.

Discouragement is a thorn that can sneak up on us at any time, depending on the surrounding circumstances. Discouragement is going to happen; it is inevitable if we are living life, especially a single Christian life. Satan is going to attack us with the thorns of life, such as discouragement. We must learn to overcome discouragement by finding a favorite Scripture or song that gives us the reassurance that life is in God's hands, and his will is best for us. I use *"Have I not commanded thee be strong and of good courage be not afraid, neither be thou dismayed for the Lord thy God is with thee"* (King James Version, Joshua 1:9).

Depression begins with disappointment. When disappointment festers in our soul, it leads to discouragement.
~Joyce Meyer

Is LONELINESS Your THORN?

Loneliness comes with life.
~Whitney Houston

Loneliness and the feeling of being unwanted is the most terrible poverty.
~Mother Teresa

It's New Year's Eve again, no midnight kisses. It's Valentine's Day, no roses from your love. It's Memorial Day, no celebration in the park. It's Juneteenth —who will you freedom dance with? It's Labor Day, no one to smear bar-b-que sauce on. It's Sweetest Day (only in

Michigan and Ohio), but not a card in sight. Then Thanksgiving rolls around and you see children, husbands, and wives just happy, happy as can be. Here we go again, another Christmas, and you have no one to buy a gift for. Then once again another year has passed and New Year's you're spending all by yourself again. You think to yourself, yet again, *I'm alone.*

As a child of God, you understand the old saying, "I'm lonely, but not alone." But man oh man, regardless of being alone, without companions, I'm still characterized by aloneness, solitary; unfrequented by people; and desolate (American Heritage Dictionary, 97).

As I write about loneliness, I think about how easy it is to get caught in this particular state, or how the thorn of loneliness can prick. For instance, when you show up for every event without a date, or a "Boo," it becomes a challenge. All your friends are sharing pictures of their husbands and children and you are sitting there twirling your thumbs sarcastically remarking, "Yea for you and yours." Then you leave and you are by yourself, with no one to share any memories with. It gets a little lonely.

"I'm not alone, I'm just lonely." That is a phrase that so often rings in the mind of so many single women. I can remember being in a workshop where a woman emotionally stated her case that she was tired of being alone. And before I could even respond to the comment, an old mother of the church proclaimed, "With God, you are never alone!"

Trust me when I say I know this statement is true, but sometimes our senior women forget that they had to grow in Christ, which then allowed them to know that there is a difference between a state of loneliness and being alone. Sometimes when we find Christ, we are so quick to forget where we came from and only want to quote where we are today.

As Christians, we have all grown in grace, and we have a

responsibility to be like Christ; sensitive and understanding to the needs of babes in Christ. So as a babe in Christ, it is important to know that there does in fact exist a difference between being alone and loneliness. Which by all means is the truth. With God, of course, we are never alone. But for the Christian woman to understand the difference between loneliness and being alone, it requires us to first grow in our relationship with Christ, and secondly to experience loneliness and understand loneliness.

Loneliness is a state of being without a companion, being apart from anything or anyone else. We experience loneliness when we experience not having that significant other, that companion to share with. Being alone means that we are in this by ourselves. That we are on life's journey by ourselves. But as Christians, we don't believe that we are trampling through the fields of life by ourselves. As Christians, we support and believe that God is the center of all creation and God is the center of our being. We believe that our being rests and rules in God our Creator. And if God is our Creator that means he is our Father, and as our Father, he is just that; Provider, Caregiver, Supporter, and Discipliner. Now sometimes it does feel like God has left us, for those of us who have grown in our relationships with Christ, because we go through moments of not feeling God's presence. Maybe he hasn't answered the prayer we've been praying for 10 years, or something has happened to leave us without the support of human connection. God never leaves us alone, although we maybe companionless.

There is an old, familiar hymn that says:

> *I've seen the lighting flashing,*
> *And heard the thunder roll;*
> *I've felt sin's breakers dashing,*
> *Trying to conquer my soul;*
> *I've heard the voice of Jesus,*
> *Telling me still to fight on;*
> *He promised never to leave me,*

Never to leave me alone.

With Christ, single women, we are never alone, but I can attest that we do have states of loneliness.

A woman who is willing to be herself and pursue her own potential runs not so much the risk of loneliness, as the challenge of exposure to more interesting men - and people in general.
~Lorraine Hansberry

Is DOUBT Your THORN?

There is nothing more dreadful than the habit of doubt. Doubt separates people. It is a poison that disintegrates friendships and breaks up pleasant relations. It is a thorn that irritates and hurts; it is a sword that kills.
~Buddha

Have you ever spent days thinking that something is not going to happen? You spend countless hours contemplating on what if it does? What if it doesn't? This belief system is what is identified as doubt. Doubt is the unbelief that something will happen (American Heritage Dictionary).

In Genesis chapter 3, we are introduced to doubt. Satan places doubt in the mind of the woman, with a few simple words. *"And the serpent said unto the woman, Ye shall not surely die"* (King James Version, Genesis 3:4). Words have so often placed negative thoughts of doubt in our minds. I remember in my early 20s, I was asked to consider modeling. I had always had my own reasons for not wanting to model, however, I mentioned to my aunt that I was going to begin pursuing a modeling career and instead of being encouraging she blurted out, "Aren't you too old to begin a modeling career?" Those words rang in my head forever, and still ring in my head today; just a few words could make me begin to doubt my own possibilities of achieving. Needless to say, although those words were repeated to me, I still

52

pursued modeling opportunities and God had it; I did all right, and I will never believe my aunt was malicious in her words, either.

Words and phrases destroy our ability to counter thoughts of doubt. You can't, you won't, how are you going to do that? You are not smart enough for that. You are the wrong color. Your hair is too this or too that. Negative words create negative thoughts, which create doubt. Doubt can prevent us from going after promotions, new career opportunities. Doubt can keep us from flirting with the cute man from the grocery store because we think we are not cute enough. First, make sure he is single before you start flirting. Women, stop trying to take someone else's husband—coveting another woman's husband is a sin (Exodus 20:17). STOP IT! (another book)

Self-doubt is a destroyer of the single woman being able to live. We must stop living in a world of self-doubt. Relationships are destroyed by doubt. I have ended relationships because of doubt, because of a lack of trust, instead of understanding that men are different creatures. I love the book *Men Are Like Waffles--Women Are Like Spaghetti: Understanding and Delighting in Your Differences*, because it focuses on the differences that exist between men and women, specifically in relationships. Now some of the relationships I needed to end because doubt proved to be true, not when differences caused doubt. But that is when it is important as single women to pray for spiritual discernment. We have to figure out what is creating doubt. Is doubt being created by self-hate, negative words, negative thoughts? Or the conviction of the Holy Spirit? Doubt is created by spiritual instability. *"But let him ask in faith, nothing wavering. For he that wavereth is like a wave of the sea driven with the wind and tossed" (King James Version,* James 1:6).

How can you remove doubt? There are three identifiable ways to remove doubt: (Strong, Supplements, 6).

Putting God to the Test
"And Gideon said unto God, If thou wilt save Israel by mine hand, as thou hast said, Behold, I will put a fleece of wool in the floor; and if the dew be on the fleece only, and it be dry upon all the earth beside, then shall I know that thou wilt save Israel by mine hand, as thou hast said. And it was so: for he rose up early on the morrow, and thrust the fleece together, and wringed the dew out of the fleece, a bowl full of water. And Gideon said unto God, Let not thine anger be hot against me, and I will speak but this once: let me prove, I pray thee, but this once with the fleece; let it now be dry only upon the fleece, and upon all the ground let there be dew. And God did so that night: for it was dry upon the fleece only, and there was dew on all the ground..." (King James Version, Judges 6:36-40).

Search the Scripture
"These were more noble than those in Thessalonica, in that they received the word with all readiness of mind, and searched the scriptures daily, whether those things were so. Therefore many of them believed; also of honourable women which were Greeks, and of men, not a few..." (King James Version, Acts 17:11,13).

Believe the Word of God
"Then he said, I pray thee therefore, father, that thou wouldest send him to my father's house: For I have five brethren; that he may testify unto them, lest they also come into this place of torment. Abraham saith unto him, They have Moses and the prophets; let them hear them. And he said, Nay, father Abraham: but if one went unto them from the dead, they will repent. And he said unto him, If they hear not Moses and the prophets, neither will they be persuaded, though one rose from the dead..." (King James Version, Luke 16:27-31).

In the word of God, he has provided us with ways and means to counter doubt. We must always take into account that God has brought us through. My cousin told me that I should date and love like I had never been hurt, and I said that's easier said than done, and her response was, "look at God's history. He has helped you to overcome heartache in the past so he can do it again." And to counter doubt as single Christian women, we must remember God's record and how many times prior he's provided, protected, and answered.

Doubt is a pain too lonely to know that faith is his twin brother.
~Khalil Gibran

Is CONFUSION Your THORN?

Truth emerges more readily from error than from confusion.
~Francis Bacon

I was speaking with a friend of mine and interestingly enough, we both were questioning a relationship she was involved with. I can still hear her asking these questions so many times. Why is he still in my life? Why won't he go away? I am so confused, I pray for him to leave because I know he's not right for me. But why won't God remove him from my life?

First, we must recognize that God does not deal in confusion; secondly, God has not removed him from our lives because our heart is not sincere in our prayer request; and thirdly, if we know he is not right for us, what else do we need God to do?

Or here is another scenario. I cannot understand why I am so broke. I am so confused as to why my money won't last. Hmmmm... maybe if you stay out of the store or stop buying things that are not within the realm of your salary, then you could get ahead financially. We must recognize that confusion within our finances can come from us not being financially responsible. God requires us to be a good steward over money, and he is not going to bless us with more when we can't handle what we have.

Confusion can also be created from the life that we live. Some of us invite a lot of confusion into our lives through clutter. We live in confused households, we drive in confused cars, we sleep in confused rooms. In other words, we allow clutter to create states of confusion. Clutter keeps us from being able to find things, identify things, and then this confusion causes us to be angry, upset, and frustrated.

Confusion is a state that we bring ourselves into. Confusion can come about through that battle of the flesh and the spirit. We refuse to do what the spirit is telling us to do and make decisions to live in what the flesh wants us to do, leading to confusion. I am just as guilty as the next single woman who needed spiritual growth to make me realize that God does not deal in the confusion of fleshly desires.

In the quote below, James Baldwin addresses the fact that you can't afford confusion in your life once you mature. Confusion can be the cause of things not being completed. As single women, we cannot afford confusion.

> *Confusion is a luxury which only the very, very young can possibly afford and you are not that young anymore.*
> *~James Baldwin, Giovanni's Room*

Is DEPRESSION Your THORN?

> *It's a recession when your neighbor loses his job;*
> *it's a depression when you lose yours.*
> *~Harry S. Truman*

Depression is a thorn that, if gone untreated, can impact every area of your life; friends, family, work, leisure. Depression can affect our relationships, causing us to lash out at people who have nothing to do with the way we feel. Depression can take us so far in that we go against God's Word because of a discontent state. Thinking about the aforementioned thorns; it's ironic to see how the fear, doubt, discouragement, loneliness, and confusion can all lead to states of depression and/or anxiety, which I touch on in the next section.

As single women, we can find ourselves in depressed states, and these are the times when we become discontent in our current state. Depression is a thorn that continually taps at your side but when unrecognized, it can become a permanent fixture. in your side. Depression can come at so many different times; during a breakup, a divorce, a job transition, etc. We have all gone through different times in life when we felt overwhelmed by depression.

I can relate that I have been in states of depression from a heartbreak or two, but I'll save that for another book. "My heart's been broken, but I recovered." A single life throws many obstacles your way that you have to experience by yourself. And that's not saying that married people don't experience things by themselves, but as a single woman, the experiences of life can be challenging when you have no one to share in that day-to-day activity.

I can remember being depressed about a job I was working in. The tension between me and my supervisor had gotten so roused up that I can remember waking up in tears because I didn't want to go to work, or not wanting to go to bed because I didn't want to have to wake up and face another day in that office. One day I remember having a meeting with her and some colleagues in which she proceeded to lean in to tell me something. She completely threw me off guard when she aggressively pointed her finger in my face. I jumped up without much self-control and said a few choice words that were completely inappropriate for work. This state of depression that I was experiencing led me to bottle up anger, which then was reflected upon my supervisor.

Of course, there is nothing like the advice from Mom, and from that day forward I began to plead the blood of Jesus over me and my office. And the blood that never loses its power allowed me to make it through a few more months until God handed me another job.

Depression can cause us to act out of what's a normal behavior for us, or it can cause us to slump into a state in which nothing gets done, life is not being lived. *"Lord, how are they increased that trouble me! many are they that rise up against me. Many there be which say of my soul, There is no help for him in God. Selah. But thou, O Lord, art a shield for me; my glory, and the lifter up of mine head. I cried unto the Lord with my voice, and he heard me out of his holy hill. Selah. I laid me down and slept; I awaked; for the LORD sustained me" (King James Version, Psalm 3:1-5).*

A few years ago, I had the opportunity to participate on a panel dealing with health and wellness. During this panel discussion, I found myself intensely taking notes on one presenter in particular. I had known Dr. John Queener as a colleague from the University of Akron. However, in this particular setting, the information he presented really caught my attention. One out of four African-American women suffers from some form of mental illness. Wow, I thought, and then ironically I was driving down the street and on the back of the Cleveland Rapid Transit Authority Bus the sign read "1 out of 5 adults suffer from mental illness." Mental illness, which includes depression and anxiety, affects our community. It affects us as women.

The statistics are a shocker that 50% of African-American women who suffer from depression go undiagnosed and receive no treatment (Queener, 2009). I know some of my fellow Christian sisters are reading this and saying, "I got Jesus and that is enough." True enough, we do have Jesus, and I am a writing witness that Jesus is enough. But I also realize that everything in and of the earth is according to God's will. *"The earth is the LORD's, and the fullness thereof; the world, and they that dwell therein. For he hath founded it upon the seas, and established it upon the floods" (King James Version, Psalm 24:1-2).*

God is not limited in his ability, and as single Christian women, we must utilize the resources that God provides us through our doctors, whether a psychologist, sociologist, psychiatrist, OB-GYN, dentist—these are all professionals that have been equipped to serve in specialized areas. And in my professional experience, I have been blessed to run into quite a few MDs that are believers in Jesus Christ. I say that as Christians, we have to stop being afraid of seeking professional help, especially when you can find a doctor that combines their medical technicality with that of their spiritual beliefs.

Depression can last for moments, days, weeks, months, years. It's important to understand that when depression hits for a long period of time, you are able to recognize the signs and seek professional help. Dr. Queener left us with nine symptoms of severe depression. These symptoms included:

1. Feelings of worthlessness
2. Helplessness
3. Hopelessness
4. Poor concentration
5. Irritability
6. Changing eating habits
7. Problems sleeping
8. Fatigue
9. Reoccurring thoughts of death

After reviewing these symptoms, I began to think that maybe I was dealing with bouts of depression, which is not something to take lightly because bouts of depression can turn into a lifetime of depression if you don't get it under control. However, it was pointed out that you are experiencing depression if you suffer from 5 out of the 9 symptoms.

I have talked with many single women about their bouts with depression, and the one thing we all say is that after a day or two, if you haven't snapped back, then you need to seek professional assistance. You can't stay in a state of depression. Have a good cry smothering your head in the pillow, or screaming and crying in the shower. But if depression is lasting for weeks on end, you have got to tackle that thorn and seek professional help. There is hope for those that are depressed because *"God… comforts the depressed"* (*King James Version*, 2 Corinthians 7:6).

> *And I always think of life like a giant wave. You know, it rises*
> *and it crests and it flies, and it's just magnificent, and then*
> *it crashes. And for a lot of people, when it crashes, that's the*
> *end, and they go down the deep, dark hole of depression.*
> *~Jane Seymour*

Is ANXIETY Your THORN?

> *Anxiety does not empty tomorrow of its sorrows,*
> *but only empties today of its strength.*
> *~Charles Spurgeon*

I can think of many nights when I have recited, *"How long wilt thou forget me, O LORD? Forever? How long wilt thou hide thy face from me? How long shall I take counsel in my soul, having sorrow in my heart daily? How long shall mine enemy be exalted over me?"* (*King James Version*, Psalm 13:1,2). I usually can't get past *"How long will thou forget me, O Lord,"* because then my mind starts wandering to the problem, the situation, or the thing that is bothering me the most. Anxiety is my personal thorn! If there is a thorn that personally affects me the most, it would be anxiety.

I am what people identify as a thinker, or in some instances, a worrier. I think all the time, and I always think that God needs my help, which then justifies me offering God my assistance with his plan for my life. I know God is laughing at me. Why does God need my help? I am non-omnipotent, non-omnipresent, non-omniscience. I had no say in the formation or the writing of Genesis chapter 1 through Revelation chapter 22. I did not create the heavens and the earth. I did not part the Red Sea with the power of my hand. I did not cause the mighty wind to blow or cease from blowing. I cannot form in a pillar of cloud or fire. Why does God need my help? I know he doesn't need my help, but that doesn't stop me from trying.

It's just as a mother with a child; when that child stops needing assistance for food cutting or feeding, it's hard to comprehend until they finally push the hand away. That is what God does to me. Every time I reach my minute hand into the situation, he pushes it away. God does not need my help! I know many of you are the same as me; you think God needs our help, which then causes us to have unnecessary and unneeded worry. *"But I have trusted in thy mercy; my heart shall rejoice in thy salvation"* (*King James Version*, Psalm 13.5). This Psalm and Proverbs 3:5,6 are just a few examples in which God says to trust. *Trust in the Lord with all thine heart and lean not unto thine own understanding, in all thy ways acknowledge him and he shall direct they paths"* (*King James Version*, Proverbs 3:5,6).

As I continue to grow in this area and ask God to help me with this classified thinker state, I have learned that overcoming a state of anxiety means that I ask the Lord, "What do YOU want me to do? What are YOU going to do? Where do YOU want me to go?" When I take "I" or "me" out of the question and replace it with "YOU" or "LORD," I am able to achieve contentment, because I begin to wait on his direction so that his will can be accomplished.

God is omnipotent, omniscience, and omnipresent. He can provide me and you with peace. *"And the peace of God, which passeth all understanding, shall keep your hearts and minds through Christ Jesus"* (*King James Version*, Philippians 4:7). I have learned to say this over and over again. God's understanding is not my understanding. God's thoughts are not mine (Isaiah 55:8-9). If I can just depend on his thoughts being best in my life, then that's when he gives me peace. I can't understand the whys, whose, or wheres but I can understand the WHO, and that the WHO is in control!

In December of 2009, the Holy Spirit was working with me and a relationship I was in. I was not sure where things were going and what was happening. A few years earlier, my mom had offered me a book,

Be Anxious for Nothing, by Joyce Meyer. It's amazing how the Spirit of God works. I wasn't ready to receive the information in the book, and I read the first page and that was it. But in December of 2009, I picked that book up and didn't put it down until I was finished, which only took a few days. Understand that the information in the book wasn't new to me, but the way that the Lord allowed Joyce Meyer to present the information allowed me to use it to reevaluate, and again put into action the things I had already learned. Sometimes we just need a jolt to get us back moving in the right direction, and that's what that book did for me.

Anxiety and depression are two diagnoses that can lead to a lifetime of discontentment if they go untreated or unrecognized. A few factors or causes for depression and anxiety are 1) Heredity - someone in your family suffers from anxiety and depression; 2) Biological - a chemical imbalance; 3) Environmental - the everyday stresses of life; and 4) A traumatic event (Queener, 2009). As single women, we sometimes suffer with ridicule for being single; ridicule for not having children because we are trying to live according to God's Word and not the world. We have experienced ridicule in so many aspects of life. It brings to mind the many sexual experiences that create a traumatic outpour in women, with molestation, rape, multiple partners, abortions; all areas that, if not dealt with, can lead to bouts of depression and anxiety.

Queener offered a few prevention and intervention suggestions to assist with anxiety and depression: 1) Prayer – a relationship with God; 2) Change your thought patterns; 3) Monitor feelings; 4) Pro-self behaviors; 5) Develop a support system and; 6) Seek out professional help.

Become a worry-slapper. Treat frets like mosquitoes. Do you procrastinate when a bloodsucking bug lights on your skin? I'll

take care of it in a moment.' Of course you don't! You give the
critter the slap it deserves. Be equally decisive with anxiety.
~Max Lucado

Discomfort in Thorns

As you have read through this chapter, you probably have been able to identify that one thorn can cause another thorn to prick or disrupt a state of contentment. Thorns are unavoidable in everyday living. One cannot avoid encountering the pricks and probes of thorns if you are living. However, it is important to recognize your personal thorns, and how thorns affect your state of contentment.

Fear can lead to a life of seclusion. Loneliness can lead to promiscuity, compulsive shopping, living a life through your children or others. Discouragement can lead to rush decisions in finances, relationships, etc. Doubt can lead to never fully trusting and enjoying a healthy relationship.

In order to pull the pricks from your side, first pinpoint the thorns that disrupt your ability to have a state of contentment. Don't forget that friends and family can also cause discontentment in your ability to live a content, single life. If you find yourself in a state of discontentment, ask God: (1) Is this hurting my well-being? (2) Did I bring this on myself? (3) Is this affecting my work and/or my personal life? If you answer yes to these questions, you are most likely in a state of discontentment.

Comfort in Thorns

"I will bless the LORD at all times: his praise shall continually be in my mouth. My soul shall make her boast in the LORD: the humble shall hear thereof, and be glad. O magnify the LORD with me, and let us exalt his name together. I sought the LORD, and he heard me, and delivered me from all my fears. They looked unto him, and were lightened: and their faces were not ashamed. This poor man cried, and the LORD heard him, and saved him out of all his troubles. The angel of the LORD encampeth round about them that fear him, and delivereth them. O taste and see that the LORD is good: blessed is the man

that trusteth in him. O fear the LORD, ye his saints: for there is no want to them that fear him. The young lions do lack, and suffer hunger: but they that seek the LORD shall not want any good thing. Come, ye children, hearken unto me: I will teach you the fear of the LORD. What man is he that desireth life, and loveth many days, that he may see good? Keep thy tongue from evil, and thy lips from speaking guile. Depart from evil, and do good; seek peace, and pursue it. The eyes of the LORD are upon the righteous, and his ears are open unto their cry. The face of the LORD is against them that do evil, to cut off the remembrance of them from the earth. The righteous cry, and the LORD heareth, and delivereth them out of all their troubles. The LORD is nigh unto them that are of a broken heart; and saveth such as be of a contrite spirit. Many are the afflictions of the righteous: but the LORD delivereth him out of them all. He keepeth all his bones: not one of them is broken. Evil shall slay the wicked: and they that hate the righteous shall be desolate. The LORD redeemeth the soul of his servants: and none of them that trust in him shall be desolate" (New Life Application Bible, Psalm 34:1-22).

God provides the single Christian woman with comfort for a contented life in Psalm 34. This particular passage address the thorns that create discontentment. First we must seek the Lord, and then he will hear us and deliver us from our fears. We are instructed that the only fear we should have is fear of the Lord. To fear the Lord means that we show deep respect and honor to God. We do this by seeking the Lord through a humble attitude and genuine worship. We purposefully build, develop, and cultivate an intimate relationship with him. We must do as the passage says, try the Lord out. In other words, *"Taste and see that the Lord is good"* (Psalm 34:8), because once we taste and see, there is no doubt that we will find that we like it (*New Life Application Bible*, 938).

God promises great blessings to his people, but many of these blessings require our active participation. We find in Psalm 34 (*New Living Version*): He will deliver us from fear (34:4), save us out of our troubles (34:6), guard and deliver us (34:7), show us goodness (34:8), supply our needs (34:9), listen when we talk to him (34:15), and redeem us (34:22), but we must do our part. We can appreciate his blessings when we seek him (34:4,10), cry out to him (34:6,17), trust him (34:8), fear him (34:7,9), refrain from lying (34:14), turn from evil, do good, and seek peace (34:14), are humble (34:18), and serve him (34:22).

CHAPTER FIVE

WHO ARE YOU IN CHRIST?

If someone were to ask, "Who are you?" "How do you identify?" or one of the most famous questions, "Tell me about yourself," what would your answer be? I don't know what it is about that question that oftentimes becomes very difficult for us to answer. We contemplate for minutes at a time some good answers. We most often give a list of our credentials, such as career, school, accomplishments, awards, honors... a list of accolades.

But almost never do we start with, "I am a child of God," for various reasons; whether we are being politically correct because it is a job interview, or whether we are scared to run someone away because it's a first date, a first encounter, or we just haven't come to grips that as Christians, that should be our first point of reference. This self-identity of being a child of God did not happen overnight for me, either. It took some time and growth that has now brought me to a point where I can identify myself as a child of God in an initial introduction, which is what I am concerned with in this chapter.

I cannot tell you to identify yourself in the workplace with an introduction of, "I am a child of God." I would love to tell you that, and do it in every interview, but I know in the world this identity might not land you the job. As Christian women, we must first infiltrate the workplace and then start spreading the gospel, because if you push too hard with the gospel on a non-believer, it might not get you in the door. In addition, always pray for discernment so that the Holy Spirit can guide your tongue in situations, such as the workplace or job interview, to know what should or should not be spoken.

How do we identify in our personal, day-to-day life? Identity has become a real focus of mine, especially in working with students, and I believe that oftentimes, because we have no grounding in our self-identity, we get lost in what I will call "sublets of identity." In other words, we sublet a situation or a person to define who we are. We temporarily lease that situation or person to place validation on our current existence. As Christians, our validation should come from security in knowing that we are children of God, and we have been created to serve his purpose.

What does it mean to be a child of God? *"For ye are all the children of God by faith in Christ Jesus"* (*King James Version*, Galatians 3:26). It means that you are an heir to the throne of God. *"For as many as are led by the Spirit of God, they are the sons of God. For ye have not received the spirit of bondage again to fear; but ye have received the Spirit of adoption, whereby we cry, Abba, Father. The Spirit itself beareth witness with our spirit, that we are the children of God: And if children, then heirs; heirs of God, and joint-heirs with Christ; if so be that we suffer with him, that we may be also glorified together"* (*King James Version*, Romans 8:14-17).

It means that you are heir to the 3,573 promises as outlined by God in the Bible (Bible Info.com). *"For all the promises of God in him are yea, and in him Amen, unto the glory of God by us. It means that you can ask anything in the name of Jesus, your brother. And whatsoever ye shall ask in my name, that will I do, that the Father may be glorified in the Son. If ye shall ask any thing in my name, I will do it"* (*King James Version*, John 14:13-14).

Christian Women's Identity in Christ (New Life Application Bible, 2133)

We are justified (Romans 3:24)
No condemnation awaits us (Romans 8:1)
We are set free from the law of sin and death (Romans 8:2)
We are sanctified and made acceptable in Jesus Christ (I Corinthians 1:2)
We are righteous and holy in Christ (I Corinthians 1:30)
We are a new creation (2 Corinthians 5:17)
We are one in Christ with all other believers (Galatians 3:28)
We are adopted as God's children (Ephesians 1:5,6)
We are God's work of art (Ephesians 2:10)
We share in the promise in Christ (Ephesians 3:6)
We are members of Christ's body, the church (Ephesians 5:29,30)
We will have eternal glory (2 Timothy 2:10)

I believe that identity plays a strong role or holds a strong place in the ability for Christian women to find contentment. I must emphasize that again, when speaking of a state of contentment, I am speaking to the Christian woman, because contentment must be achieved through a real heart-mind-soul relationship with Jesus Christ. This is for those women who have skipped the chapter on contentment and thought you'd start reading here.

Understanding how contentment is achieved also helps to understand how discontentment arises. From the two previous chapters, we know that thorns or issues with fear, loneliness, doubt, anxiety, depression, and confusion, can lead to discontentment. But what about identity?

Self-identity is such a major factor when it comes to being a woman and being single (that does not mean that women who are married or men who are married or single don't deal with identity issues, they do). But as single women, not knowing who we are in regards to self-identification can impact multiple areas of our life. Women who have not come to grips with accepting who they are become easy traps for outlets to define them. They allow sublets or false prophets or spirits of the flesh to define them and give them self-identification, as John speaks of.

> *Beloved, believe not every spirit, but try the spirits whether they are of God: because many false prophets are gone out into the world. Hereby know ye the Spirit of God: Every spirit that confesseth that Jesus Christ is come in the flesh is of God: And every spirit that confesseth not that Jesus Christ is come in the flesh is not of God: and this is that spirit of antichrist, whereof ye have heard that it should come; and even now already is it in the world. Ye are of God, little children, and have overcome them: because greater is he that is in you, than he that is in the world. They are of the world: therefore speak they of the world, and the world heareth them. We are of God: he that knoweth God heareth us; he that is not of God heareth not us. Hereby know we the spirit of truth, and the spirit of error (King James Version,* I John 4:1-6).

Issues of identity can stem from several factors. For instance, Jonetta Rose Barras suggests in her book *Whatever Happened to Daddy's Little Girls? The Impact of Fatherlessness on Black Women,* men first fall in love with their mothers, a daughter's encounter with her father is the first sight of love for her. But when a father is missing from the home, or in the home but not present, it creates this void in a woman's life. This void affects the life of a woman on many different levels. For instance, if there has never been someone to reassure this woman as to who she is and what level of respect she deserves, it leaves room for sublets to take the place of her true identity, specifically in Christ.

Other identity issues for women are created in environments in which their self-worth and/or self-esteem is not reassured. There are women who grow up in households or environments that are sometimes verbally and/or physically abusive, which then lends itself to an attack on a woman's self-worth. These situations can only be countered when a woman begins to identify with a positive self-worth, sometimes using positive affirmations. As Christian women, our positive self-worth comes from the fact that we are daughters of the Most High, who has given us authority and dominion over the earth (Genesis 1:28). When we begin to question our self-identity, we begin to open doors or make way for "sublets" to counter who we are.

Very briefly, let's look at some examples of sublets that replace a Christian woman's identity in being a child of God: beauty; material wealth (money); career; others. In reviewing a few of the sublets that we sometimes use to identify ourselves, make sure to understand that they are not negative at the surface. These sublets only become negative when we allow them to define us and be the pure existence of our identity.

The Sublet of BEAUTY

"Favour is deceitful, and beauty is vain: but a woman that feareth the LORD, she shall be praised" (King James Version, Proverbs 31:30).

As Christians, we don't talk much about our identity being defined in our beauty. I don't think we really talk about beauty because we have been taught that as Christian women, we should be modest. I remember I asked a group of students what do they define as beauty. Now these were both young men and young women, and of course, most began with beauty is defined by what's on the inside and not what's on the outside.

Then I shared with them as I am sharing with you, "What happens when we Google the word beauty?" We get a number of women that are of European descent, with Beyoncé and Rihanna sprinkled somewhere in the mix. Not once did I get a picture of a heart, emotion, or feelings on the inside. Society, or the world, has attached a standard of beauty that puts women constantly on alert for what classifies or characterizes them as beautiful. Our hair, our clothes, our body shape, our hands, our feet (all things on the outside) have become or set a standard for what beauty is through media or self-prescribed images, outlined by the people we are closest to. Although the media provides a distorted view of beauty, or a cookie-cutter image of beauty. We must understand that beauty comes in all shapes, sizes, colors, and ages. Beauty is not defined by one set standard, and as Christian single women, we must learn to embrace our beauty, but not allow beauty to become our crutch for self-identification.

Thinking about this concept of beauty and how it ties into identity for the Christian woman, my mind goes two different directions. First, understanding that it is okay to accept and embrace our beauty, but secondly, we can't let our beauty define who we are. Growing up in the Church, I noticed how no one ever referenced physical appearance when it came to teaching life lessons. Instead, we always go to the lesson on fornication, drugs, alcohol, music, dressing modestly/being covered—presenting our bodies as a living sacrifice. *"I beseech you therefore, brethren, by the mercies of God, that ye present your bodies a living sacrifice, holy, acceptable unto God, which is your reasonable service"* (King James Version, Romans 12:1). But never a life lesson on understanding beauty and how it impacts you as a woman. I think as Christian women, it is important for us to understand the physicalness of beauty.

The Bible describes many women that were beautiful or fair. What is interesting is that the Bible references its description of beauty to the physical appearance (to look upon) or countenance, which according to Webster's dictionary, is defined as "appearance; the expression of the face. The face or facial features." Countenance can also be referenced as an encouraging look or expression, but still, it is something you see.

Sarah

"And it came to pass, when he was come near to enter into Egypt, that he said unto Sarai his wife, Behold now, I know that thou art a fair woman to look upon" (King James Version, Genesis 12:11).

71

Rebecca

"And it came to pass, before he had done speaking, that, behold, Rebekah came out….And the damsel was very fair to look upon, a virgin, neither had any man known her: and she went down to the well, and filled her pitcher, and came up" (King James Version, Genesis 24:15-16).

Rachel

"Leah was tender eyed; but Rachel was beautiful and well favoured" (King James Version, Genesis 29:17).

Abigail

"Now the name of the man was Nabal; and the name of his wife Abigail: and she was a woman of good understanding, and of a beautiful countenance" (King James Version, 1 Samuel 25:3).

Bathsheba

"And it came to pass in an evening tide, that David arose from off his bed, and walked upon the roof of the king's house: and from the roof he saw a woman washing herself; and the woman was very beautiful to look upon" (King James Version, 2 Samuel 11:2).

Tamar

"And unto Absalom there were born three sons, and one daughter, whose name was Tamar: she was a woman of a fair countenance" (King James Version, 2 Samuel 14:27).

Queen Vashti

"To bring Vashti the queen before the king with the crown royal, to shew the people and the princes her beauty: for she was fair to look on" (King James Version, Esther 1:11).

Esther

"And he brought up Hadassah, that is, Esther, his uncle's daughter: for she had

neither father nor mother, and the maid was fair and beautiful" (*King James Version*, Esther 2:7).

Job's Daughters

"And in all the land were no women found so fair as the daughters of Job: and their father gave them inheritance among their brethren" (*King James Version*, Job 42:15).

Notice how the reference of beauty for these women is a subset of a bigger picture in their stories. The women are referenced as beautiful or fair, but their identity falls in a larger picture of who they are. For instance, Sarah was beautiful, but her beauty was a subset to her bearing the lineage to the 12 tribes of Israel (Jacob). Rebecca was beautiful, but her beauty was a subset to the fact that she would be the mother of Jacob, fulfilling God's promises to Abraham. Rachel would be one of Jacob's wives to bear him two sons, Joseph and Benjamin, who later procreated to produce two generations of the tribes of Israel. Esther's beauty is that she was the king's soon-to-be wife, sent forth on a larger mission as ordained by God to save the Jews from mass genocide. Out of a marriage that started as adultery between David and the beautiful Bathsheba, King Solomon was born and the lineage of Jesus Christ. And yes, as in David, God has the power to still bless our disobedience.

But what happens so often is, instead of us embracing our beauty for God's larger purpose, we use our beauty as a means to get ahead, hurt others, and think that we are the cat's meow. Our beauty cannot be who we are. Our beauty must be a subset instead of a sublet of who we are. It must complement and enhance the larger purpose that God has for us in being one of his children.

The Sublet of MATERIAL WEALTH

Videos, radio, YouTube, Pandora, TV, Social Media . . . we can hear and see the money, the bling, the cash, the wealth everywhere. There is always something buzzing in our ears about material gain. In the '80s, Madonna hit the listening audience with:

> Living in a material world
> And I am a material girl
> You know that we are living in a material world
> And I am a material girl

Today, our music has become a glorified, high-end sales market for material ownership. Trinidad James captures our unconscious singing with:

Gold all in my chain; gold all in my ring; Gold all in my watch. While Keri Hilson featuring Keisha Cole and Trina hit us with:

> If you think you impressin' us with your ice and your dub
> Poppin' bottles in the club, get your money up
> 'Cause I ain't your average girl, I've been all around the world
> If you wanna wow me, then get your money up

> Get your money up, boy, get your money up
> I wanna see somethin' bigger than an armored truck
> Get your money up, boy, get your money up
> You gotta throw somethin' bigger than a hundred bucks

> Now slide, slide one of them Black Cards
> Make the Pacific Ocean be part of my backyard
> If you ain't gonna pay, don't be screamin' out, "Hey!"
> I'm an independent honey, I get money all day

> Now slide to your bank account, all the cash, throw it out
> If you ain't yellin' dollars and diamonds, I gotta walk it out
> Know what I'm talkin' 'bout? You steppin' to the baddest
> Got millionaires standin' in line wishin' they had this

Take me to Paris, buy a lotta carats
Christian Louboutin boots, bags, and more carats
You want average, well, this the wrong section
My girls need the check, so we headin' in their direction

Get your money up, get your money up
Stop playin' with yourself, get your money up
Get your money up, get your money up
Stop, now let me see your booty drop

Then Big Tymers goes on to say in "Still Fly":

Hoppin' out the platinum Hummer with the platinum grill
With the platinum pieces, and the platinum chains
With the platinum watches, and the platinum rings

And Future says in "Honest":

Everything exotic I'm just honest
Gold all on my neck I'm just honest
Gold bottles on bottles, I'm just honest
100,000 on watches I'm just honest
Coupes all on coupes, I'm just honest
I'm a rock star for life, I'm just being honest
Got a check on me right now, I'm just being honest
And I'm driving foreign coupes, dash 200
My diamonds ain't got flaws, I'm just honest

Material wealth is not only glorified in our music, but it is seen in so many reality TV shows: *the Real House Wives of Atlanta, Beverly Hills, Love and Hip Hop, Basketball Wives.* When we listen and believe such lyrics, it causes us to begin to ground our identify in material wealth instead of material wealth being a subset of who we are.

Not everyone will be a billionaire or a millionaire; however, as a single woman, you can maintain a healthy lifestyle if you are obedient to the word of God. "*This book of the law shall not depart out of thy mouth;*

but thou shalt meditate therein day and night, that thou mayest observe to do according to all that is written therein: for then thou shalt make thy way prosperous, and then thou shalt have good success" (King James Version, Joshua 1:8).

Terry Anderson stated in a sermon entitled "When a Nation Rejects God" that, "If you are exposed to an idea long enough it becomes normal." For the world around us, normal is defining yourself by material gain.

"No man can serve two masters: for either he will hate the one, and love the other; or else he will hold to the one, and despise the other. Ye cannot serve God and mammon" (King James Version, Matthew 6:24). We have become so guilty of making money our god. Possessions have become the definition of who we are. I remember growing up hearing the phrase "Keeping up with the Joneses." I had no idea what it meant until I started listening to women tell me about their debt based on the purchases they had made, which were beyond their income bracket. When you allow money to define who you are, it becomes your god. As Christian women, we must look at money, possessions, and wealth as a gift from God to be used for his kingdom-building.

Now do not get me wrong, I like nice things, and I like to purchase items of quality. But I have learned that only identifying in wealth gives me no substance or dimension. *"But seek ye first the kingdom of God, and his righteousness; and all these things shall be added unto you" (King James Version,* Matthew 6:33). If we are obedient to the word and will of God, he will give us all the material wealth we need. But when we understand that it comes from him and not of our own accord, we are able to make it a subset of our identity instead of the basis for our existence.

The Gospel duo Mary Mary summed it up best in what it means to have material wealth as a subset of identity instead of a sublet of identity.

You're so fly, you're so high
Everybody 'round you trying to figure out why
You're so cool, you win all the time
Everywhere you go, man you get a lot of shine

You draw like a magnet, better yet I have it
Everything you wear people say they gotta have it
From the sweat suit to the white tee to the Gucci
You can probably say people wanna get like me

You see her style, you think she nice
You look at her whip, you say the whip tight
You look at her crib, you thinking she's paid
You look at her life, you think she's got it made

But everything she's got, the girl's been given
She call it a blessing but you call it living
When it come to money she can be a hero
She writes them checks with a whole lot of zeros

But what you don't know is when she get home
And get behind closed doors, man she hit the floor
And what you can't see is she on her knees
And if you ask her she'll tell you

It's the God in me, it's the God in me
It's the God in me, it's the God in me
It's the God in me

The Sublet of CAREER

In 2007, a few weeks before my PhD graduation, I was at a bridal
shower when I heard a family friend introduce herself over and over
again as Judge such and such. I could not understand why she insisted
on using her title at such an informal gathering. And from that, I
began to pay attention to individuals who were caught up in their

titles. In education I deal with it daily, if you don't reference some as doctor, they have the potential of getting livid. The world has caused non-Christians and Christians alike to get caught in the sublet of identifying yourself by career and/or title.

As a single woman, I cannot tell you how many times I have heard this question: "What does he do?" But in a Christian household like mine the question was: "Does he believe in Jesus?" I am even guilty of asking my friends, "What does he do?" At one point, I had become conditioned to believing that a man's career is his be all and end all; whether he was self-employed, a business owner, or a PhD. I'm not saying they are all like this, but what I began to realize is how many of them were defined by their title or their careers. I began noticing in conversation they had nothing else to talk about except themselves, which became a sure sign that their career was a sublet of their identification.

In I Samuel 9-31, we are given an example of a man who became so wrapped up in his title and position that he lost sight of his identity in God. Due to the fact that Samuel's sons proved to be corrupt judges, the elders of Israel demanded that Samuel give them a king. God gave the people what they wanted, and Samuel anointed Saul as king. Saul's appearance was great for a king, for he is described as tall and good-looking. But his character was often contrary to God's commands for a king. It's important to point out that Saul was God's chosen leader; however, if you are chosen by God, it means you can't do or achieve anything without God.

Throughout his reign as king, Saul had his greatest successes when he was obedient to God. His greatest defeats came in his acting on his own accord. Saul let the position of king identify him instead of it being a subset for God's use. Saul's own choices cut him off from God, and eventually alienated him from his own people.

> *Samuel also said unto Saul, The LORD sent me to anoint thee*
> *to be king over his people, over Israel: now therefore hearken*
> *thou unto the voice of the words of the LORD....And Samuel*
> *came no more to see Saul until the day of his death: nevertheless*
> *Samuel mourned for Saul: and the LORD repented that he had*
> *made Saul king over Israel (King James Version,* I Samuel
> 15:1,35).

When we let our career or title dictate who we are, we end up engulfed by the need to always stay in this position, no matter the cost, just as King Saul. Because of his own self-will to stay king, he lost the anointing of God. Isn't it better to be a child of the King in which *"all things are possible" (New International Version,* Matthew 19:26) than to have a title that does not alone have the power to achieve anything?

The Sublet of OTHERS

Can you fathom a time when you allowed someone else to define who you are? I can think of numerous times when I observed individuals using others to define themselves. As women, we get so caught up in letting others define who we are.

Children

As a parent, oftentimes a woman may find herself living life through the lens of her children. It's usually not intentional, unless it is a lifetime movie, but it occurs because somewhere along the line, this woman lost sight of who she is. She instead takes on her sole role as mother—provider and nurturer. How many times have you heard the saying, "She is living the life she missed out on through her daughter"? Is this a true statement for some? Yes, for varying reasons. Some women had children early, so they were not able to live or do things they wished they could have, so they live vicariously through their children's social lives of friendships and dating. Other women believe they missed out on something career-orientated, so they send their children into a field in which they wish they had pursued. Our identity does not come from our children. Our children do not define who we are, just as our parents don't define us. But they do have a strong impact in shaping and molding us.

There is an old, familiar story that comes to mind when I think of a mother and how her actions displayed future issues with her child. *"And the LORD said unto her, Two nations are in thy womb, and two manner of people shall be separated from thy bowels; and the one people shall be stronger than the other people; and the elder shall serve the younger"* (King James Version, Genesis 25:23).

The New International Life Application Bible states that Rebekah was an initiator, and whenever she saw a need, she took action, even though the action was not always right. Rebekah's initiative of offering a common stranger a drink caught the attention of Eliezer, the servant of Abraham, who presented Rebekah as a wife for Isaac. However, Rebekah's initiative became tainted and self-willed when she planned ways for Jacob to overshadow his older twin brother, Esau. *"And Isaac loved Esau, because he did eat of his venison: but Rebekah loved Jacob. And Jacob sod pottage: and Esau came from the field, and he was faint: And Esau said to Jacob, Feed me, I pray thee, with that same red pottage; for I am faint: therefore was his name called Edom. And Jacob said; Sell me this day thy birthright. And Esau said, Behold, I am at the point to die: and what profit shall this birthright do to me? And Jacob said, Swear to me this day; and he sware unto him: and he sold his birthright unto Jacob"* (King James Version, Genesis 25:28-33).

Rebekah loved Jacob more than she loved Esau, and her favoritism was shown in her deceitfulness towards Isaac. While Isaac was on his deathbed, Rebekah convinced Jacob to fool Isaac into giving Jacob his blessing instead of Esau, the older son. Not only did Rebekah use deceit to fool her husband, but this craftiness was a demonstration of how women can become so wrapped up in their children that they lose sight of the bigger picture. The bigger picture was that God was in control, without the help of Rebekah.

As a parent, it is also important to understand how children become defined by our actions. For instance, Jacob was a chip off the old block. Early on in life, Jacob coerced Esau into giving him his birthright for food. Jacob was just as cunning and crafty as Rebekah.

Friendships/Relationships

Often times new relationships/friendships can also impact our identities. Week one, You spend hours on the phone talking with him. Week two, every day it's a new date. You are so excited because you have found someone who shares everything you want in a mate. Week five, "What's up, girl? Haven't seen or heard from you. I know you got a new man, but don't forget about us!" This scenario can go so many ways, but it gives an idea of what could and can happen. First, you have gotten so wrapped up in this new relationship that you lose sight of your life before and after him (who you are). Or secondly, his attentive ways become so controlling that you forget your own self-identity. Everything becomes about what he wants, what he needs, what he has to have instead of your needs and wants. You no longer desire anything for you, it's all about the desires of his heart. And thirdly . . . this scenario can turn out great! You rectify the situation with your girlfriends by calling them and bringing them into the circle of friendship. You give them an adequate amount of time, just as your mate. This was only a few weeks of excitement that has now diminished (not in terms of your like/love for him) because you realize that you have a life and a self outside of your relationship with him.

Although any one of these three scenarios could play out, it's often that women find themselves in scenario one or two. Women find themselves in the trap of identifying their selves or their lives by their mate or significant other. As a single Christian woman, it is important to understand that your value and self-worth is not defined by someone being on your arm or in your presence. Your self-worth is defined in the way you carry the confidence that comes from knowing that you are a child of God.

Not only do we as single women lose sight of our identity in our mates or dates, but we also lose our identity in our friends. We wear the same clothes, we drive the same cars, we live in the same houses. Please understand, it is okay to have similarities; but when your identity becomes overpowered by their identity, it creates an issue with your individual self-esteem.

When a person desires to be someone else, that is an indication that something is missing from their lives. To take on another's personality, especially a friend, is indication that a person has not come to grips with who they are. As a public speaking coach, one of the things that I emphasize when I am training is that a student must learn to deliver using their own personality. Students are going to pick up some of my delivery techniques, just as I have done with others who taught me, but their personality is not my personality. They must come to understand just as I have who they are as a speaker, and what does and does not work for them.

The problem comes when a student emulates the way I speak, the hand gestures I use, but has not come to grips with how to incorporate themselves or their personality into the mix. When this happens, an individual loses sight of their own identity and begins to take on the identity of others. We begin to use the same voice inflection, the same hand gestures, drive the same car, live in the same building. If you know who you are in Christ, then you are not at risk of taking on the personality of others. Instead, you will take on the characteristics of Christ.

Either you can be like Christ or you can have Heda trying to emulate your entire life, as in the 1992 movie starring Bridget

Fonda and Jennifer Jason Leigh, *Single White Female*. You become so engrossed with another's life that you begin to take on every aspect of their life. You lose yourself in someone else.

The Sublet of the PAST

How many single women are still holding onto the past? Past mistakes? Past relationships? Past accomplishments? Past successes. We are still using the past to define who we are today. STOP IT! The past does not define who you are. It may have contributed to where you are, but it does not define who you are. We are carrying so much baggage from our past that we can't see our future. We have used so much of the past to dictate the future. STOP IT!

I say STOP living in the past when it comes to mistakes, failures, or accomplishments, when you find that you have a tendency to use those to define you. However, it is important to understand how the past affects your future and who you are. The past becomes a problem when we dwell on it use it as a crutch for not moving forward. The past should be used to assist in defining your future and mapping your future. But of course as humans, we have a tendency to be so caught up in our past that we can't move forward. We can't believe that God would forgive us for such terrible sins. How could he? It's because you can't get over it and you have allowed it to define who you are instead of it being a mistake or achievement that was just a part of your life. Don't wear your past as your wardrobe. Instead, use your past as an old shirt that you have taken off and have now thrown away.

PART II

LIVING PROOF OF
CONTENTMENT:
I'M SINGLE, SO WHAT?
THE TRUE STORIES

I'm Single, So What? captures what it means to embrace a state of
singleness. Being single is not always easy, acceptable, or comfortable.
Part one of the book presented detailed information on how to achieve
contentment according to the word of God. This information defines
and outlines what it means to be in a state of contentment.

Reading of achieving contentment and seeing it displayed in the
lives of others are two different things. Part two of the book enables
you as the reader to understand that contentment can be achieved even
when you are in a state of singleness. To illustrate that, as women,
we can live a life of contentment; not meaning that all days are good,
happy-go-lucky days. Sometimes some days take a little more prayer
than not to get through your state of singleness. However, it's in those
times that you also realize that because of your relationship in Christ,
you have contentment.

Part two is the real women, real stories, the true stories of being
single and being content. I interviewed 13 women from different

demographics to illustrate that being single and being content are possible. As you read each story, reflect on the principles that you learned in part one and see how these women use them to assist in their life of contentment. Use their stories as an example so that you too can find joy in singleness. Use their stories to give you life application skills on being single and enjoying it.

These are real stories of single women sharing their ups, downs, joys, sorrows, pains, and regrets, as they express how they overcame or achieved contentment in being single. Each story exhibits a real-life example of *I'm Single, So What?*

HEATHER'S TRUE STORY

In 1961, the Shirelles sang:

> Mama said there'll be days like this,
> There'll be days like this Mama said
> I went walking the other day,
> Everything was going fine,
> I met a little boy named Billy Joe
> And then I almost lost my mind
> Mama said there'll be days like this,
> There'll be days like this Mama said
> My eyes are wide open
> But all that I can see is,
> chapel bells are callin' for everyone but-a me
> but I don't worry cause
> Mama said there'll be days like this,
> There'll be days like this Mama said
> And then she said someone will look at me
> like I'm looking at you one day,
> then I might find
> I don't want it any old way,
> so I don't worry cause
> Mama said there'll be days like this,
> There'll be days like this Mama said
> Hey! Don't you worry,
> Mama said mama said
> Hey! Don't you worry now.

Hey, Mama, it is 2020 and I'm still having days like this. I thought days like this would mean one or two days, not two, three, five, or ten years. I just want to scream! But probably if I screamed out loud, someone might think I was a little crazy, so that's why usually when the frustration of single life hits I just scream in the shower.

I was going to say throughout my life, but I think I'll say throughout the last few years that I've wanted to settle down, it seems as if chapel bells are calling for everyone but me. I go on social media, Facebook, Twitter, Instagram—everyone is posting pictures of their spring wedding, summer wedding, fall wedding, winter wedding, destination wedding, Vegas wedding, church wedding, Justice of the Peace wedding; that's all I see is wedding after wedding. Pastels, flowers, rings, candles, that stupid little pillow . . . oh yeah, the ring bearer pillow, just kidding. I'm really not bitter about marriage or love. I think it is the most beautiful thing, especially when God is in the midst. However, some days I just can't take it, other days I couldn't care less.

Let me tell you, it's not easy being single. Here I am, a woman in her forties, never married, no children. What's wrong with me? I have to ask. Did I miss the boat? Did I miss the one? Did he pass me by? Did I ignore him with my pickiness, wanting my type, my career, my independence, or as Mya Angelou speaks, "My haughtiness." I know I look all right (at least that's what they say). I've never been shy of a date, but maybe I'm dating wrong, I don't know.

My girls and I have decided to implement the advice of Dr. Henry Cloud's book into our lives, *How to Get a Date Worth Keeping*. I had already begun to do a lot of the things he suggested in the book, just for self-discovery of me. Like, for instance, there is one guy that I'm really interested in. We have been casually dating (not sexing or sleeping together) for over 11 months, however, he's on a spiritual journey all his own (which, knowing his past, he needs). But throughout this time period I made up in my mind that I was never going to let a man dictate my relationship pace based on his place or space in life. What do I mean by that? In other words, I am not going to sit, hope, and wait on him to commitment as I let others pass me by. No, I decided after past experiences of dating this one for 2 years, another one for 3, that I would casually date others (create a list, as Dr. Cloud suggests) and go out as often as I like with whom I like.

Now it's funny how honesty has attracted more and more to this newfound experience. I refuse to play games of any sort. My speech goes like this: "Hey, I'm casually dating about 2 or 3 others, however, there is one guy that I care about. But if you are willing to go out occasionally, with no serious commitment, no sexual intimacy or relations, just getting to know each other, then I'll go." I think this becomes a challenge for the men also to see if they can move up the list, because the response or something similar follows with, "Can you add me to the list?" By all means! And then I wait on the next date.

Ironically, the dating thing can become tiring and disappointing, because of course not everyone is Mr. Romeo or close to it, so it's a numbers game, as Dr. Cloud states, and you have to weed out the bad seeds (or the ones just not for you).

I'm sure you are now questioning, how does multiple dates illustrate contentment? It illustrates contentment because in this realm of multiple dating, I'm not looking for a husband—no, I'm enjoying life, experiencing new things, learning new things, learning others, learning myself. My goodness, if nothing else, in the words of a dear friend, at least I'm getting a chance to eat. She had 32 dates in one year all premised on the fact that she didn't know how to cook and she needed to eat, but prior to that she had spent five years in a dead-end relationship.

Although I have always been content in my single state, I've had good days and bad days. No one likes the idea (or at least, most people) of spending a lifetime by themselves. And with no children and no husband, some days I do get a little down. I remember my last birthday, and I was having one of those days. I heard from a friend of mine—of course, a male friend (because as single women, we have plenty of male "friends"). And his first question was how are you, birthday girl? And immediately I could feel my eyes fill with water as I began to explain, today sucks. I'm single, no children . . . and of course he gave me a reality check that I could be much worse off. I was breathing, I was alive. Look at all I had accomplished at this age. And of course, all I could hear was yada yada yada...until he threw God into the mix. There's something about just hearing the words *God, Jesus, the Holy Spirit.* It brought what I like to call that "peace beyond understanding" and that "unspeakable joy." Now don't get me wrong, I didn't snap out of the slump immediately, because deep down I felt some type of way. And then of course I had to see about 10 couples that day. His remarks were, don't let the outside fool you, they may be miserable in their relationship. But after I took a minute to pray and reflect on the blessings that I did have, I began to process my contentment and understand that this is only my current state.

I don't ever want anyone to be confused that contentment does not bring about emotions that make us cry, laugh, or hurt, but contentment allows us not to focus, dwell on, what we don't have. To my sisters, I need you to clearly understand that contentment for me was not and is not an easy process, but it is a necessary process. Especially now that I am older and still single. I believe in a God-ordained marriage, and I believe that God has someone for me; I have not lost that hope. However, I understand that my contentment comes from me knowing that God has a plan for me right now, and there are things that I need to accomplish as a single woman first.

I can't answer the question, what happens if I don't ever get married, because I am not thinking like that. However, I am not fantasizing that every man is my husband, like some of us do. Instead, I'm enjoying life. I've even become addicted to cooking shows, because I love to eat. The one thing I do know is that I can cook with Snoop and Martha and I learned a few years ago how to make a mean 30-minute meal, thanks to Rachel Ray. So whoever God has for me, he will eat well.

For the Single Sister, from Heather:

"Single sisters, stay in the will of God!"

I'm Single, So What? Heather's journey to spiritual contentment.

JANAE'S TRUE STORY

The church members said he was her knight and shining armor. He would be perfect for her. A few years older, a minister of the gospel, previously married, with two teenage children, tall, dark, and handsome. Who could ask for more? She laughs and giggles. "I should have asked for more." Because as it would have it, the knight in shining armor traded in the white horse he rode in on.

Janae remembered how she was smitten by her ex-husband. They shared prayer time, Bible study sessions, and long talks—before the road got rocky and the marriage ended. She was single, no longer married, living alone with two children.

After speaking of her single life, Janae quickly began to reflect on how she felt single even when she was married. "I often felt as if I existed in my marriage alone as a single woman." Disappointment watered in her eyes as she spoke of the many times she felt as if all the responsibilities of the marriage fell on her shoulders. "It was if I was dancing solo without a partner. I always felt as if I was single even when I was married." But in spite of dancing alone in her marriage, Janae has a great co-parenting relationship with her ex-husband. "I learned that in co-parenting, I have to compromise a lot to make this thing work. I have to give a lot, as we usually have to do as women, and that isn't to say that my ex-husband is not a great father, because he is. But women always give more because we are the nurturers, we are the mothers." I would be inclined to believe that Janae has one of the best co-parenting relationships that I have observed. It is great how well the two parents work together for the benefit of the children.

"It is what it is!" Janae smirked. "Oftentimes, as women, we work the hand we are given?" Janae was resourceful. "I did what I had to do. Even now I pray my way through everything." Janae admits that she has accepted being single and she is coping with her single state. However, candidly, she knows this is not a place she wants to exist in for the rest of her life. In spite of a rocky relationship, Janae wants to marry again, as she blurts out, "I'm not meant to be single." However, she oftentimes questions whether she should or should not stay single, given some of the challenges that she faced in her marriage. "In singleness, you learn to rely solely on yourself. However, the challenge comes; some days you are tired of being single. Tired of all the responsibility, yearning to share your accomplishments, goals, and life with a companion, a husband, a mate."

But since Janae has been single, she's achieved some great success. She graduated with a Bachelor of Arts in English and a Master's of Science in Education. Janae is that single woman who also takes pride in maintaining a healthy weight program. She jokes and says, "You know how sometimes in our singleness we let ourselves go, so I try to keep myself healthy, spiritually strong, and mentally stable." Janae admits that it's tough being single, especially when you want to marry again, and that she is trying to master dating without marriage being the ultimate goal and to learn from her past mistakes. Of course, I told her to read *How to Get a Date Worth Keeping*. Being single has allowed Janae ample time to grow in her faith, to have a stronger prayer life. "The way I look at the world is a lot different. I've stopped living by society's standards of what the good life is. Doing what works for me is living God's plan for my life."

Going from being married to single is not an easy task for Janae. In the past, financial security was one of the things that made being single difficult for Janae. She shared with me a time in which she was in school and trying to raise her family on a graduate assistantship. "I've always been able to hold down a job, but trying to go to school and raise a family was a struggle. But thank God I made it through!"

Janae uninhibitedly tells me that the thorn that pricks her the most is loneliness. "I believe that God didn't make me to be single. I wasn't created to be single, because I have so much love to give. I am very loving in nature." With this loving spirit, Janae reluctantly admits, like so many Christian women, that her thorn of loneliness oftentimes leads to fornication. "I often find it difficult to abide by the principles of Christianity, being single, especially when it comes to sex." However, as a Christian single woman, she admits that she often has to pray about these challenges and that she has learned to be transparent with the Lord about her challenges. Janae stays in constant prayer, asking God to change her circumstances so that the challenges don't combat her life and remain a constant obstacle. "In changing my circumstances, I am referring to progressing my relationship in a way that leads to marriage."

The thing I came to realize about Janae as she told her story and we spent hours talking, is that her heart always belonged to another man, her current relationship. The man she dates today so happens to be the man she dated before she married her husband. But because she wanted to marry, and as she claims today, her "soul mate" was not ready to marry, she found herself rushing God's plan instead of waiting on him to do his work.

Janae's eyebrows rose as we began to discuss her level of contentment in her state of singleness. "Hmmm, contentment; not 100%. It depends. I feel like I'm in a state of contentment, but looking at it from a biblical perspective, my state of contentment does not satisfy how God would have me live as a Christian." From that I concluded that Janae is still trying to find a continuous state of contentment that has not been achieved because of her "circumstance."

For the Single Sister, from Janae:

"The single life has its ups and downs. I would say being single is not for the weak or the faint at heart—from a biblical perspective. Therefore, I suggest that as single women, we stay in prayer about our situations and about that peace and contentment that we need to get through each day. Knowing that God is and can be our source for everything we need; if we truly believe and practice what it means to have faith."

I'm Single, So What? Janae's Journey to Spiritual Contentment.

TRINITY'S TRUE STORY

She never would have thought she'd still be single at this age. She never was the type of woman that had her life planned out in terms of marriage. Some women have it all figured out. "I'll find my husband in college; marry by the time I'm 25. Have my first child at 30 and then send them off to college and live my life with my husband to the fullest, traveling, seeing the world at 50." That was not Trinity! But Trinity was the woman who always knew the exact details of her wedding. And it may have been because she played every role in a wedding she could play as a woman. She was a wedding coordinator, a bridesmaid, a flower girl, and a hostess. And how could she forget the number of times she attended someone's bridal shower? So it was only natural for her to map out every detail of her own wedding.

But in spite of knowing how she wanted her wedding to go, from the opening song to the closing prayer, she never thought about actually being married until just recently. What changed? In her mid-thirties she thought to herself, "I'm single! I never planned on being married early, but I never thought I'd be this age and not married." And yet today, she is still single. But never in her wildest dreams imaged she'd be without a husband at 44 years old.

One of the things that helped Trinity embrace her current state of singleness is that she came from a single-parent home. Her mom and dad divorced when she was a young child, so it was always her, her mom, and her brother. Although her father was an active part of her life, she still was reared by a strong single mother whom she watched embrace her singleness.

Because Trinity's mother married in her twenties, she never pushed her children to marry early. Her mother was from a generation when women married early, or otherwise they were thought of as an old maid. Her mom emphasized the opposite with her children because she didn't want them to experience her story. Her remembered how often she'd hear her mom say, "You have time to fall in love." According to Trinity's mom, she fell in love every other week. Trinity's mom told her she had time; but who knew she had this much time!

Over the years, as a single woman, Trinity has had many self-revelations, but the biggest was that in 2013 she "still" was single. There are many women who get caught up in the fact that something must be wrong with them because they are single. Trinity even felt that way. "Why am I still single? Is it something I did or didn't do?" But after taking a step back, it's obvious that God is still working things out in her life, and working on her. One of the biggest areas Trinity struggles is in submission to God's will in her relationships. She has a habit of trying to self-manipulate situations, putting her hands in place of God's hands, trying to change him and the situation in her favor. But over the years, Trinity has learned that self-manipulation doesn't work when you are trying to live in accordance with the will of God for your life.

Over ten years ago, Trinity was engaged—briefly, but still engaged. Trinity knew she wasn't ready for marriage because she never seemed excited about it. When people would comment or ask, she'd just nonchalantly respond. Truthfully, she didn't even love him, or probably like him, but had put herself into a situation full of manipulation and lies. Believing she was a strong, confident woman who knew "game" never would have imagined she'd be a part of such a relationship. Her ex-fiancé lied so much that he would tell you the sky was green when you were looking at the sky and knew it was blue. This led to trust issues for Trinity that she had to pray her way through constantly in order to regain trust in those she loved, who she knew would never lie to her, but because of him, she thought everyone to be a liar.

Trinity had to depend on the only trust she had to get her through, and that was her trust in God. "Without a personal relationship with Christ, I don't know how I would have ever overcome such a situation." Trinity remembers vividly the time she called her ex-fiancé another woman answered the phone, proclaiming herself proudly as his girlfriend. She remembers instantly her heart dropped to her feet. The pit in her stomach hurt like a knife was digging straight through her flesh. This was also the time that Trinity was preparing for an exam in school. Needless to say, the exam didn't go so well. Trinity's bed became her crying board. She'd lie on the side of her bed in a fetal position and cry until her eyes were swollen beyond recognition. But daily she had to live a life in the public as if nothing was going on around friends and family. But as God does, he gave her the strength to overcome. Her smile shined brightly and her heart slowly opened itself up to love again.

Trinity admits that sometimes she carries some of this baggage with her and has to stay in constant prayer so as to not take it into new relationships. But this was that turning point, when Trinity admits that no man is worth a life of discontentment and restlessness. Without a test, what is the testimony? So Trinity was thankful for her experience because it gave her a testimony to tell others, especially her single sisters.

Trinity has learned over the years and through this experience to listen to the Holy Spirit, because when he speaks, listen! In this case, instead of listening to the Holy Spirit and being in tune with the will of God, Trinity listened to friends and ended up in a mess of a situation. But thank God he brought her out! Trinity believed that if she had gotten married during that time, either her or her fiancé would have ended in jail or dead—not saying which one, but that just calls your attention to how toxic the relationship was.

Well, needless to say, today Trinity is still single. Trinity refuses to put her life on hold as she waits for Mr. Right. Instead, she enjoys spending time with the Mr. Right that now comes along because from each date she's learned what she wants and doesn't want.

Trinity admits that "this dating thing" is a little difficult. She remembered once chatting with a married friend, trying to decide which is easier or harder, being single or being married. Of course Trinity argued that being single was harder, because when you are married, you are learning the quirks of one man, unlike in dating, you weed out the quirks of many.

As a married Christian woman, you are living under the covenant of Christ, which makes it scripturally appropriate for you to have as much sex with your husband as you want; you can partake all day, all night, all week, all month, all year. But when you are single and trying to live according to the word of God, premarital sex is a no-no, so you have to suppress, back down, control all those feelings—yes, all those good, sexual feelings that we all have—or at least Trinity admits that she has.

Single women have to be in tune with the Holy Spirit, in order to weed out all those unrighteous men who don't mean single women any good.

Trinity believes that another setback for single women is that they have to deal with married women believing every single woman is interested in their husband. Married women, that is far from the truth! "Hate to be the bearer of bad news, but not all single women are interested in your husband. Sorry for the reality check!" Now there are some women who are scandalous, just like some men, but not all single women are looking to be disobedient to the word of God and defile the marriage bed.

Another challenge of being single is that people automatically think something is wrong with a woman because she is not married. It is time to realize that just because a woman is single does not mean she is crazy, can't cook, doesn't clean, doesn't work, is lazy, and the list goes on. It just means that for the Christian single woman, if she is choosing to have a mate, she is waiting on God to send someone in his image and to love her as Christ loved the church, unconditionally. Trinity believes that God has her Adam, for she knows that it is *not good that man should be alone* (*King James Version*, Genesis 2:18)

Personally, and maybe because Trinity is single, she does not believe that there is anything wrong with being single. Being single has allowed her so many opportunities and experiences that may not have been afforded her had she been married or had children early. Not being married made it a little easier for her. For instance, unlike some of her colleagues, during her state of singleness, Trinity graduated with three degrees by the age of 34, a bachelor of arts, a master's, and a PhD.

She has been able to accept who she is, which she reflects in her knowing that she is a child of God. As a single woman, Trinity has been able to grow in her relationship with Christ. She has been able to travel, enjoying life as a single woman. Over fifteen years ago, Trinity was able to pick up and move across country because she only had herself to answer to, except of course God. Being single allows Trinity the freedom to move from job to job, city to city, and only worry about her financial security and not that of her husband or children.

Trinity has developed an appreciation for being single. She will eat breakfast, lunch, and dinner by herself. Because Trinity travels so much with her job, it forces her to be by herself. And being by herself has helped her to come to love herself, because if she can't love herself, then who else would? "I love myself!" Trinity giggled as she reflected on the number of times she's traveled.

As we began to conclude the interview, Trinity joked, "It's funny, I guess I have learned how to be content in my state of singleness." Trinity went on to say, "I can't change that I am single, so why not embrace it? Why not run your first 5k at 40? I did. I've embraced a lifestyle of exercise and healthy eating." In 2007, Trinity lost her dad, and through his sickness, she learned that her dad was diabetic, along with her paternal grandmother and her aunt, so she made a conscious choice to make a lifestyle change with her eating. She also realized that if she wanted a potential husband to even look her way, she would need to make sure that he had something to look at. "God formed me; however, he didn't give me this body to defile." So with that, she began watching what she ate and exercising, usually working out anywhere from 3 to 6 days a week, depending on her schedule. "I think recently I've become a workout junkie, but I love it, because it's making me a better me, and it's helping to relieve the sometimes daily stress of being single. Because when you are single, with no husband or children, you are your sole provider, and sometimes it's a little scary." Christian single women who seem to believe that after 20 you are no longer hot can be just as sassy in their 30s, 40s, 50s, and 60s, if they take pride on the outside as much as they pride themselves on their hearts being right in Christ.

Trinity believes that it is important for Christian single women to be conscientious of how many younger women may be watching their testimony, which is why she chooses to embrace her single life, because in her everyday life, whether it's her staff at work, church, or her community, she is careful to watch how her contentment in singleness may affect them. For instance, she states, "If I hadn't learned to embrace my singleness, how could God use me to tell a

23-year-old that it's okay that you are not in a relationship? Being by yourself doesn't make you any less of a person."

There are ups and downs in being a single Christian woman, Trinity admits. Sometimes she is lonely, and just wants to have a good, solid date, the kind with flowers. But when dates aren't knocking down her door, she takes a prayer break and asks God, "What's next during this time of singleness?" It's not easy being a Christian single woman that wants to date; that is something Trinity will debate with her married friends forever. However, it is a little less difficult to embrace the "good" in being single. "Find something that works best for you; read and study the word of God. *"Study to show thyself approved unto God, a workman that needeth not to be ashamed, rightly dividing the word of truth"* (*King James Version*, 2 Timothy 2:15). "Maybe it's time to pick up that old hobby of photography. Maybe it's time to run a marathon, enroll in school, travel the world, or find a purpose-driven job. Why not write? I did! From speeches, to plays, to books, to poems, to newspaper articles, to grants. I've been writing, and it's been great!" Trinity smiled.

For the Single Sister, from Trinity:

"Single sisters, grow in your relationship with Christ, because when you grow in your relationship with Christ, you begin to use his pruning of life experiences to teach you how to be content."

I'm Single, So What? Trinity's Journey to Spiritual Contenment.

CHELESA'S TRUE STORY

Recently divorced and she meets the man of her dreams; personality and looks to die for. She never thought he'd come from a different ethnicity and spiritual background. Day after day she wrestles with this relationship. Being divorced for a few years, she gave dating a try, only finding herself really caring for the man of her dreams, and ironically, he recently called and she had the same giddy feelings, as Chelesa laughs, sharing details of the phone call.

During, during the time they dated, she began to grow stronger in her faith as he distanced himself from the faith. She began committing more and more time to raising her children, and her church work. Suddenly, after every date with the man of her dreams, she found herself having a reoccurring nightmare. Can contentment actually come in a nightmare? Weeks went by, and Chelesa continued to have this dream, until one night the dream became so real that when she woke, she had dug or clawed the skin from her own arm. Every night Chelesa had dreamed that she was being buried alive, but no other night ended like the last night, when the dirt began to pile high on top of her as she aggressively tried to claw her way out. Chelesa leaped out of her bed to find herself kneeling in prayer as she delivered a prayer of surrender to God. "Lord, whatever it is that you will have me to do, I'll do it. From this day forward, I dedicate myself to you and your work. If it be your will, I ask that you suppress all my desires to date."

Chelesa never dreamed in a million years that God would answer so soon. A few days later, the man of her dreams willingly walked away. Chelesa had found contentment in a dream. It was through prayer and her maturity in Christ that she realized there was more to life than concentrating on being married again.

Married at 25, divorced at 33, and blessed with two children, Chelesa never thought she would be single for more of her life than married. Chelesa married young because she came from a generation of women that believed that if she were not married by 24, then she would be considered an old maid. So Chelesa felt like she was under a certain amount of pressure to marry, because that was the expectation. And of course, mutual family friends introduced the couple. But after eight years of marriage, Chelesa felt that she could no longer continue being married to an alcoholic. She jokes and says, "I should have known he was an alcoholic when he showed up at our wedding drunk."

Chelesa also admitted that she knew it was time to leave her ex-husband when she found herself fantasizing about what it would be like to be with other men. But walking away from her marriage was not an easy thing to do for her because she never wanted to be labeled as the divorced woman; in her mind, she feared that people always labeled the divorced woman as the loose woman, always after someone else's husband.

Years later, of course, Chelesa no longer has that fear. She also shared with me that she purposefully kept herself away from married men because as a single woman, she never wanted anyone thinking that she wanted their husband. Being single was not always an easy task, Chelesa admits. Just like most single women, there were many days that she found herself lonely. But she made a conscious effort to stay involved in her church work, and more importantly, study and pray continuously, and not focus on not having someone.

Although loneliness would strike, Chelesa feared getting involved with someone, because like most women, who wants to be hurt or disappointed yet again? "But as I grew spiritually and closer to the Lord, those fears began to disappear. I got over them. I became more comfortable in who I was and who I belonged to. And I think knowing and being in Christ just made me feel good about myself and comfortable with who I am. Really, it's only because of my faith." She smiled and said, "I haven't thought about fears of being single in years. I'm just thinking about them because you are asking about them now."

Then Chelesa shared a story that many single women have shared with me over the years of how single women have been accused of being a lesbian because they do not have a man on their arm. "I was able to deal with it because I knew it wasn't true. I had no problem with identifying with me being a fairly attractive heterosexual woman with a nice figure, so I never let it get me down. But it hurt to hear people say that, just because of not having a man. But you move on because time will prove itself."

Another common thread for Chelesa and most of the true stories is the issue of finances for single women. Chelesa refused to take a second job as a single mother and she never did, but she attributes it to her trust and faith in God and her belief in the ordinance of tithing. She admits that early on she would fall short in her tithing commitment, but it was also those times that she fell short in her finances. Chelesa proudly shared that she and her children never wanted for anything. "I always wanted to live in a fairly decent neighborhood because of my son, and my concern for his safety with gangs and violence. So I am thankful that God afforded me the opportunity to raise my children in fairly decent neighborhoods."

At 70 years old, Chelesa is proud of the accomplishments she has achieved as a single woman. She believes that God has blessed her ministry because she is single, and she has been able to devote 80% of her time to do the work of the Lord and the other 20% to her children. She laughs as she says, "Maybe my children got 30% instead of 20."

Chelesa remarkably speaks of how being a single woman has allowed her to depend totally and completely on God for everything; her decisions, her finances, and any task that has been thrown her way. This woman is amazing! In her ministry, she has worked with hundreds of youth at her church and the community. Chelesa believes that her state of singleness is what has allowed her to share in the lives and mentor so many young men and women that a married life would not have afforded her. She has taken Christian counseling and Bible classes, and attended, hosted, and facilitated numerous workshops. She has excelled in her career as a professional woman and still is employed and utilized at the age of 70, she giggles, "Because my mind is sharp." She attributes her greatest accomplishment to her being a single mother and that God has allowed her the privilege to nurture and raise a beautiful and intelligent Christian man and woman! "Raising my kids was my number one priority, and one thing I never did was have a man that I dated around my children." And then she hysterically laughs, "Probably because I only seriously dated one man after my ex-husband. I just believe that single mothers should not entertain male company in front of their children—unless the relationship is progressing and moving forward to marriage, that is."

You can see the light in Chelesa's eyes when she speaks of her children. Chelesa says she faced a few challenges in being single, and one was raising her children without their father in their daily lives. "I wanted my kids to understand that I could not be their father. I could only be their mother and I was going to be the best mother that I could. also found myself having to be fair to my children in a lot of instances because I worked with so many young people; I never wanted my children to feel that they were not a part of my life, or that they were being set aside because of the needs of other children."

Chelesa is proud that she has been able to live a God-filled and God-directed life as a single woman!

For the Single Sister, from Chelsea:

"Have a right relationship with the Lord and pray much! In other words, TRUST GOD FOR EVERYTHING! The one thing is be content in the state you are in, but also remember that you have to continuously be in fellowship with the Lord in order for him to be able to minister to your spirit so that you can be content; not saying that every day will be easy, because there are times when that old nature will get to turning in you. But if you are constantly praying for his guidance and not your own, and being still and letting him minister to your spirit, that's how you stay content until he gives you a husband or says you're not going to be married again. Now I am content with what God has given me; but if I didn't have my kids, I wonder. In my single life, I have lived by John 15:7, and I ask that all single women live by my favorite Scripture: 'If ye abide in me, and my words abide in you, ye shall ask what ye will, and it shall be done unto you.'"

I'm Single, So What? Chelsea's Journey to Spiritual Contenment.

KURREAN'S TRUE STORY

Truly a Holy Spirit-directed, honest, fulfilling interview. Surprised, but not shocked, as Kurrean opened the interview with prayer. It is just a sentiment of how her life is a testimony of now living a life directed in God's will. Married for 10 years, Kurrean, a divorcee, admits that in the past she lived life to please herself and others instead of pleasing God. "How can you please God when everything was about self, me, and I?" I thought this as I listened to her share her story. But so often as single women, just as Kurrean, we lose contentment because we live life to please others instead of pleasing God.

Kurrean openly admits that on her wedding day, she knew her marriage was not right because as she stood steps away from the exit door she heard a voice say, "It's not too late, you don't have to do it." That voice being the voice of God. But Kurrean went through with the marriage anyway. She even remarked that she knew it was wrong when her pastor refused to marry them, with her future husband being divorced and outside the faith. But flesh got in the way, the desires of self. At that time, Kurrean was in the church and actively involved in the church, and had been sexually intimate with this man and figured that if she married him, the premarital sexual sin would not be added to her account, so she went through with this marriage that she knew was outside the will of God.

Kurrean says that her self-revelation of being single came in the raising of her son and being a single parent. Kurrean's son is from a previous relationship. "Being a single parent allowed me to know that I was a single woman, because I didn't have any input from a man speaking into my son's life. That's how I realized I was single." This same revelation that made her realize she was a single parent is the accomplishment of which she is most proud. "My son is an accomplishment because I realize that the Lord allowed me to take a ride as he grew him up. I always thought I was driving; it wasn't until I got older that I realized that God was allowing me to ride along." She admits that being a single parent has not always been easy; as mother and son, they have gone through some things. But God brought them through it, and she thanks God for her son.

Being single has offered Kurrean flexibility to serve on the evangelism team and other boards. In her state of singleness, God has allowed her to be around people that are mothers, grandmothers, and sisters in Christ who have raised their children to love the Lord with God's speed.

It is so in your face how God has had a hand on the life of Kurrean, in spite of her many "self-detours." I listen intently as Kurrean reflects on an experience she had at 17 or 18 years old. It was altar call, as usual, and Kurrean made her way to the front of the church. But something was different about this time; it was as if the Lord had pointed and called her out. As she listened to the prayer, she began to feel the floor shaking. Not sure if anyone else around her felt the same sensation of the floor shaking, something overwhelmed Kurrean, and in spite of "self and flesh" causing detours, Kurrean knew she had been set apart for God's work. "I really think if I had waited on the Lord, I think my life would have taken a different direction. I think God would have allowed me to be comfortable because that is where he placed me. I did detour, but he always brought me back."

Kurrean is grateful to finally be at a place in life where she is comfortable in her own skin. In fact, she shared with me how someone had recently remarked to her about how comfortable she was in her own skin. "I thought to myself, hmmm, that sounds just about right." She smiled. Coming from a place in which she based a lot of her decisions on what others thought and her needing to be validated by others and receive accolades from others that were 9 times out of 10 untrue, she is comfortable in who God has created her to be.

Kurrean smiles as she shares she has found her confidence in herself "because of who God is and because God is so merciful and kind and patient that he would take my grungy life and make something of it, and to share that with others that I would not have the luxury if a man were in my life." Kurrean believes that a man in her life would only be a distraction to the person that God has created her to be. She would have been centered on that man, instead of centered on the Lord. "I believe that God has set me aside to be just for him and not married."

When Kurrean stopped listening to others and became confident in herself through Christ, she realized that she no longer had to listen to other people tell her that she was supposed to be married. Instead, she believed that she got beyond that fleshly desire of most of her relationships and realized that it was not love, but the flesh. "You don't know what love is until you come to love the Lord; that's when you can measure what love is, and that's when you know it has nothing to do with flesh."

Just as with marrying her husband, Kurrean believed that a number of struggles as a single woman, especially when it comes to men, dating, and relationships, has been based on her want. "When I was out there it was about me, it was about what I wanted to do. But when you get beyond that me thing, that's when you realize that what God has done for you becomes real. It's like rushing water, a cleansing, and it comes from his throne. Not a leaky faucet, but a fountain that floods you with his love."

All outward appearances make you think Kurrean has it all together, but she was not shy in telling me that there are times that she has fallen but because of Christ's love, she has gotten back up again. Just two years ago, Kurrean decided to try dating again, but the flesh got weak and she slipped. However, the guilt of the Holy Spirit ate her up. "Losing my relationship with the Lord wasn't worth it; not those two minutes." We both laugh. "But thank God that he gives us a conscience, that he doesn't allow us to be comfortable in our sin. When you are on this side of Zion you will have those desires, but when you think about God's agenda, and whether it will please him, it makes you push back," Kurrean confirms without doubt.

Just as many other people, I've been guilty of blaming a single woman's contentment on the fact that she has a child, so I asked Kurrean just to see what her response would be if she did not have her son. Would she still find herself content? She answered, "I don't think not having my son would have made me feel any different about being single because in spite of my detours, God had to get me back to knowing him."

And it is so obvious that Kurrean's contentment comes from her knowing Christ and having an intimate, personal relationship with Christ. "I've never been caught up in being single because I have always been comfortable moving to my own beat. Even when I was out there trying to mix, I never actually fit in. I would go to a small bar, have a drink and sit in a corner. If I talked to someone, fine; if I didn't, that was fine too. Majority of the time I was trying to make myself fit. Outside people made me feel as if I needed to have a man. I never said I needed a relationship. Everyone I dealt with, they forced themselves on me and I took it as if this was the way it was supposed to be."

There are some single women who have been labeled as needing a man on their arm no matter what the man looks like, does, or anything, because he is only for a date. Kurrean made it perfectly clear that she is not one of those women. She is comfortable being by herself and does not have a problem going anywhere alone, although this is a challenge for some single women. Kurrean is focused on keeping herself daily in tune with God's will, and it is something that she doesn't take lightly, which has also contributed greatly to the confidence she exudes when she walks in a room.

Kurrean makes it plain that although she is content and comfortable in being single, she has had thorns or struggles. She admits that finances are not her thing, and she is not alone on that one. She does not plan or budget. Admittedly, she shared that she is frivolous with throwing money away. Kurrean is praying for the day when this thorn exists no more and she is able to be a good steward of money, as the Lord instructs, and help those in need, because in spite of being a tither, poor money management lands her in the bushes.

Personal fear based on past experiences and past cycles have landed Kurrean facedown on the thorn bush. She shared a story with me in which she remembered going on a date with a "gentleman"— well, for lack of a better word. At some point in the evening, the date walked away from Kurrean. During this time, another man made his way to engage in conversation with Kurrean. When the date returned, he asked to speak with Kurrean outside. She proceeded to follow and within seconds she found half her body stretched over an outside balcony with his hands around her neck, speaking the words, "If I ever see you talking to someone else I will kill you." Kurrean admits that she thought this was love, that jealousy exemplified love in her eyesight and ironically, her ex-husband and many men she dated were possessive. "The man who gives you static is the same one who is out there doing wrong." She smiles and says, "True love is not accomplished until you meet Jesus."

Kurrean has become so content in her single life that when I probed her about would she ever marry again, she said, "Only if the Lord says so. It would have to be his guidance, his approval, his will. I have tried this on my own and I have fixed this on my own." The church is the bride of Christ, and Kurrean already has her groom. It reminded me of my guilty hand trying to fix and manipulate things, like God needed our help.

For the Single Sister, from Kurrean:

"Love yourself and realize how much God loved you to send his only son to die for you. When you come to the realization that someone sacrificed their only son for you, then you can love yourself because of what Christ did for you. It's because of what Christ did for you that you have to love yourself."

I'm Single, So What? Kurrean's Journey to Spiritual Contenment.

LAUREN'S TRUE STORY

Like most women, in her early 30s, Lauren faced the scare of chronologically aging and attempted to take pro-creation into her own hands. However, there was no success. Lauren had made a conscious decision not to use birth control with the man she was engaged to in hopes of becoming pregnant, because she figured he loved her, so why not do the next logical thing and have a baby together? She's thankful that God had mercy on her and did not allow that plan to prosper, because the relationship ended in a breakup when her ex- became an addict. Since then, he's turned his life around and has recently married. But that didn't affect Lauren one bit. To this day, she remains friends with her ex.

After the breakup, years later, Lauren found herself single and not wanting children, so around age 41 or 42, she decided to have tubal ligation. Lauren joked with her father about the possibility of adoption; however, that idea never came to pass.

Now she is sixty-three years old, never married, and has no children. Has Lauren really been able to achieve contentment in a state of singleness? Yes! Today, with no desire to marry or have children, Lauren has filled the void of marriage through church work, and the love of family and friends.

As a young woman, Lauren dated one guy in particular and thought they would marry and have children, but as time went on, thoughts of marriage became thoughts of the past. After years of casual dating and no real serious boyfriend, Lauren still has no regrets with or for non-commitment. Nevertheless, after hearing that her parents had never divorced but they lived apart for years because of her dad's alcoholism, I asked Lauren does she think that impacted her ability to be in a committed relationship. Lauren answered, "I believe that did have something to do with my ability to commit. Look at my mom, who was a strong woman and would rather live that way than deal with the negative. She went out and continued to work and raise her children. I didn't have children, but I found so many things that replaced that. I don't believe there was anyone that I could commit to. I had relationships, but sometimes I caught myself getting close and I would back up, and didn't feel bad about it because that's what I wanted." Lauren's mom and dad always maintained a good relationship, even with the living situation. On visits to Cleveland, her dad would always stay in the house with her mom.

I joked with Lauren and said, "In your heyday, I bet you had a lot to deal with working in the church as a single woman." Of course, she did! Women, we all know that sometimes the church (God remove these demons) can become a mating ground, worse than the club scene, for singles, when we ignore the will of God. Lauren shared with me how so many times she'd have to make phone calls to the homes of members and before she could get a hello out, a jealous wife would go off on a rant. But that did not stop Lauren from doing the work of the Lord; she shook those situations and many more off, and continued to be grateful to God for the ability to share with others her gift of making both men and women feel comfortable with her singleness, no matter the situation.

Lauren realized she was single when she didn't need anyone to make her feel whole, and today she is enjoying being with herself. She found herself at a point that if someone broke up with her, she was cool with that. Lauren says that being single afforded her the opportunity to participate in softball full-time, work full-time, go bowling 2 or 3 nights a week, and when she was outside of the church, she assisted with party planning. But now she has replaced partying with churching. Being single, Lauren has spent more time doing the things she enjoys. "I can give it my all, and don't have to worry about cooking and homework."

She admits that she has a habit of being selfish, because when she wakes up, it's all about her. She is learning how to share her time and taking on the concerns of others. "I really had to work at thinking about other people and giving them time." Being single and the oldest sibling allowed Lauren the time and energy to nurture her siblings that would not have been there if a husband were in the picture.

Lauren admits that some of her contentment came in the form of watching others. "There were so many of my friends that had been married, separated, and divorced, with children, and in bad relationships," that she didn't want or need the negative aspects of relationships to complete or make her feel completed. Instead, Christ has been the impact on her ability to be content in singleness.

As a young woman, Lauren admits that she was not well-versed in Scripture, which caused her to have a much harder time in finding contentment. But the desire to be better caused her to learn more about the Lord. And that desire and yearning for Christ has enabled her to become a better and stronger woman. "Because I had help! Without hesitation, my relationship with the Lord has been able to help me get through and become more committed," she exclaimed.

Singleness has not always been easy for Lauren. She can recall days when she suffered from bouts of depression because of medical issues, and there was no way she could have gotten through those tough times without the Lord. Tough times with medical issues are also the times that make you miss having someone, Lauren confesses. "There are situations where you want to have someone there to talk with and share the results of your exams. Someone just to say, baby, things happen, but it's going to be okay, and we are going to get through this."

Being by yourself in these tough times can cause your mind to play tricks on you, allowing the enemy to infiltrate your thoughts. Singleness can also bring about loneliness. There were times on the holidays when Lauren's family was there but she was by herself and lonely. She made sure to let me know that the holidays were the only times of feeling lonely that remotely got to her, because if she needed a date, she could get one. My sentiment exactly.

Although Lauren has never married, she has been involved in an intimate 14-year companionship. "He is not actively involved in the Church, but he has not deterred anything with my faith, because he is a believer, and there are times we sit and talk about the Lord." She laughs, "We even watch T. D. Jakes together."

Of course, me being me, I had to ask how she feels about being sexually active. Lauren responded, "It does not affect me any kind of way." It's a story of true friendship; he has been there for her, and she has been there for him.

For the Single Sister, from Lauren:

"First of all, you have to love the Lord, which helps you to have a self-love. And if you love the Lord and yourself, there is something that will make you want to do more for the Lord, do more for yourself, and do more for other people. As long as you are alive, there are always going to be things that are going to come up to stop you from being the woman you should be or want to be. But you can make it! You can survive the things that come your way!"

I'm Single, So What? Lauren's Journey to Spiritual Contenment.

DELILAH'S TRUE STORY

Delilah had finished all of her course work and her graduation was approved. However, because of her husband's insecurities, she postponed walking across the stage to receive her master's degree for two years. She says her husband left, her daughters say she put him out in January of 1991. Either way it goes, she proudly walked across the stage four months later to receive her master's degree in hand. And since then, she has been blessed to live a life full of God's favor. This woman is amazing. She has traveled all over the world, gotten two daughters through college, and paid off a mortgage early, all while being a Christian, content, single woman. Being married, she suggests, would not have allowed her these opportunities because she married a man that was submersed into his own self-satisfaction. He even commented to his daughter once, "Don't you want me to be happy?"

Her divorcing her ex-husband allowed God to create opportunity for financial security. She shared with me how her ex-husband had a liking for cars and was an impulsive spender. If there was money, he loved old cars to fix up, so he would buy a Corvette or the latest gadget when it came to music; and it didn't matter the cost. However, he never finished fixing the old cars, so Delilah always drove old cars when she was married. "With two incomes, we always had jacked-up cars," she hysterically laughs. "But as a single woman, I've driven a Cadillac."

Having a husband enables a woman to step back from a lot of the household fixer-up responsibilities, and that's one thing Delilah admits has been hard for her. She feels like she is always at the mercy of someone else when it comes to fixing the furnace, updating technology, and repairing the house. She jokingly admits she could probably read and learn more, but she just doesn't feel like it. So instead, she pays someone to do a lot of the things that her ex-husband used to take care of, because she confirms that, like some men, he was good at mechanics, electronics, and technology. Yet, still with this, Delilah says leaving her husband allowed her to regain her voice and find security in her intelligence that she was so used to dummying down because of his insecurities.

Today, whether she has lost or gained weight, Delilah likes herself. She prides herself in having a foundation in Jesus Christ, great friends, and strong family ties. She even has opened her house up to so many relatives. She jokes that she is always raising someone's child. These are the things that keep her from focusing on being single. She also says that she uses defenses that keep her from focusing on being single, defenses of staying busy, like work, school, and others. "I'm so busy dwelling on those things that I don't think about myself. When my kids were young, I focused on them. You don't have time to think about what you don't have because you are busy working on what you do have."

It wasn't always like this! Raised as a Christian young woman, Delilah found herself entering into marriage at the age of 21, trying to wipe out the sins of fornication that were being committed with her then boyfriend. Delilah experienced life. She'd had a steady boyfriend from the age of 14 until she met her ex-husband. Never a drinker but on occasion or two, she partook in casual weed smoking, like so many high school and college students.

At age 20, Delilah realized how far left she had gone that she decided to work in a co-op program in order to reel herself back in. This would not be the last time that Delilah took "self-diagnosed treatment" into her own hands. After her divorce, and being in a state of depression, Delilah checked herself into a hospital. But when the doctor came in and threw his feet on the bed and said, "You don't belong here, you are not having a nervous breakdown," she knew her diagnosis was wrong. Although there were no signs of a nervous breakdown, the therapy session allowed Delilah to talk about not only the betrayal of her ex-husband in his infidelity, but allowed her to deal with losing her mother as a child, and the treatment of her stepmother. Like any therapy session dealing with grief, these sessions helped her to deal with the anger stage in the seven stages of grief. It allowed her to stop being angry and start being more in control, which ultimately led to her becoming an obsessive planner. She had a 2-, 3-, and 5-year plan. This plan helped her get over a 19-year marriage, separated at 37 and divorced at 40.

Delilah's ex-husband deceived her from the beginning; there were a number of things he neglected to tell her during the friendship/dating stage. For instance, that he had two daughters, had been married, was ten years older than Delilah, and never enrolled in college classes like he had claimed. But by the time these things came to light, Delilah was far into the relationship and her feelings for him. She felt like to him, she was a damsel in distress, and he was a knight in shining armor, because he was so unlike her ex-boyfriend. He was mature, and possessed qualities that her ex-boyfriend didn't have. She truly cared about her ex-husband. But that doesn't stop her from admitting the belief that her ex-husband was a rebound. She believed that if she had waited six months before entering into a new relationship, she would have never married him. She also admits that she should have listened to the voice of the Holy Spirit on two occasions: the day before the wedding, when she had a dream that she ran away from the wedding, and another time when she saw him in a light that was indescribable but frightening.

Years passed, and the relationship got worse. Two or three years before the relationship actually ended, Delilah remembered telling her pastor, "There is a black hole in my chest, and I am afraid to look down because I might see it." She remembers driving home hoping he wouldn't be there; that's when she knew she had to do something to save herself, and the only way to save herself was to end the marriage. She believed that she had enough faith and self-confidence that whatever the outcome, it was better than where she was.

She speculated he was unfaithful, but then she found a letter to prove his infidelity and her suspicion, so she knew it was confirmation to leave because she refused to stay with a man who cheated on her. That was the one thing she told him in the beginning of the relationship; she could forgive a lot of things, but she could never forgive infidelity. In her mind, this was the self-revelation that led to her state of singleness. Although she didn't want her daughters to be labeled as children from a single-parent home or her to be labeled as a divorcee, she knew it was over. "I was never afraid of being single, I just hated the defeat. I got an 'F' in that course, and I'm not taking it again." Delilah thought she would marry again, but within those first five years of her divorce she was more concerned with controlling her environment and making sure she didn't lose her home, her girls didn't get off track, getting things in order, and keeping a job.

With the financial shape that she is in today, no one would know that her mortgage was five months behind at the time of her divorce. So when men came her way, she didn't want to make time for them and as time passed, she was financially secure and doing so well that she questioned most men's ability to bring something to the table. Delilah not only has herself together professionally, but she is a very attractive woman who runs from the attention of men.

Sometimes Delilah finds herself ingrained in the phobia of asking the Lord, "What is wrong with me?" and the negative thoughts of not truly believing that a man is interested in her. "I think I can't tell the difference. I don't know why. My father was very supportive and made me feel great as a person—competent and capable. But I realize a mother teaches you other kinds of things." Delilah lost her mother at an early age. "Now that I am old and gray, I ask the question of why would someone want me, and then I don't want to give off the wrong vibes. I remember one of the ministers put his arm around me, which made me uncomfortable, and immediately I asked what I did to make him think he could do that."

And I'll be the first to say that she is not that type of woman. She is not aggressive, and you will never catch Delilah sashaying up to any man.

She admits that in order for her to ever date, she would have to be introduced. But the problem with that is that her friends don't introduce anymore because she's turned down so many. And then she was caught up in her list: was he ever married, did he have children, and she knew that she had children but her preference was not to have a man that did, because she had been in a marriage in which she was the stepmother and mother, and being the best at both of those is draining because you raise your stepchildren as your own. And so with that it was seemingly impossible to find a date over 40 that had never been married or didn't have children.

She also admits that dating is hard for her because she is not going to make the same mistakes, and she refuses to have sex with someone she is not married to. And how do you convince a man that you are not going to do that at her age? She admits, "Sex is important, but it's like you know when you need your hair washed but you go another day without washing it." At first I had no idea what she was talking about and then it hit me; with washing your hair, you go one more day and your hair doesn't look bad. With sex you go one more day without having it and you don't die. Like a couple of the divorced women interviewed admitted that early on they missed sex, and Delilah was no different. "Early on in my relationship, I missed sex. It grieved me that I would not have that relationship again. But getting involved in my job, the church, raising my children . . . sex was not a back-breaker. I'm not going to grow another head and I am not going to go out looking for someone."

At around 46 or 47, she did have a friend that was very much into her, but Delilah, being a little naïve, didn't realize it. However, it was in this relationship where it became decision time. She would have to risk being alone if she expected to remain holy in her relationship and walk with the Lord. She confirmed her decision and walked away. "Why risk my salvation?" But to this day, the two of them remain good friends.

As a 60-year-old Christian, successful, single, career woman and mother, Delilah does see retirement in her future. However, she has already begun to make plans for what's next. She recently told her pastor that she was going to work for her two or three days a week. "I don't have a problem telling people what I want." As women, we age, and Delilah confesses that she does have a problem with trying to figure out what she will do when she's in her 70s or 80s and can't take care of herself. The same questions that we all raise as single women: "Will I insist upon staying in my own home and have my children become my parents? Will I go into assisted living?" Those are the things that frighten Delilah in this aging process, becoming older and falling prey. Although she mentions these things as concerns, she doesn't dwell on them, because she is thankful and blessed to be in good health. She reminisces about a friend of hers who died from Lou Gehrig's disease and all the suffering she went through. "So when the enemy brings those thoughts to mind I pray to take those out." She nods and smiles.

For the Single Sister, from Delilah:

"Stop saying I can do bad all by myself! If you change that message, then you begin to feel worthy of having good things that you can give to yourself. Change the message in your head that you can do good by yourself. That's the message to tell yourself. I would like for single women to know that God fills in the gaps. There is never any promise that everything will be good, whether you are married or single, but as a single person, accepting singlehood allows you to say to God, I am going to trust you, even with that, and he fills that place if you allow him to. You will still cry and ache because the human existence is to be mated, but you won't long for or be discontent because it hasn't happened for you."

I'm Single, So What? Delilah's Journey to Spiritual Contenment.

JOY'S TRUE STORY

Her mother thought he was "the one." When Mom thinks he's the one, 9 times out of 10, he's the one. Joy even thought he was the one. But "the one" turned out to be "the wrong one," and so have so many other dates that have followed. But let me share a few thoughts about Joy's "the one" because he and their situation is representative of what so many of us as single women deal with.

Some of us choose to stay while others of us, like Joy, eventually walk away. He's the "almost" perfect guy, or at least he's perfect for you. He calls, he dates, he shares, he does everything that you ask, only to discover that he's doing those same things for someone else. Yes, he did the unthinkable, he cheated. How did Joy discover? She professes it was nothing but God warning her. Her house phone rang, and he offered to answer the phone because that is the relationship they had. She answered his phone, he answered hers. He had a key to her place, she had one to his place. But this particular time she said, "No, I will get it upstairs." As she picked up the phone, she heard his voice mail playing (private eye speculates that he had called his phone and didn't hang up properly and so the phone rang back). She continued to listen, like we do as curious single women, and she heard another woman's voice clearly identifying herself also as his girlfriend. After playing the message over and over again, Joy confronted him; let's call him Tony.

Now I know you are thinking that Tony came up with a good

excuse; nope, not at all. Tony was so dumbfounded and caught in the act that he couldn't even think on his feet and lie. Joy broke up with him, of course, but after "cordially" meeting with the other woman, she forgave him and he cheated yet again. Joy realized that this was something in his system, and she didn't know whether he mistook her kindness for weakness and thought that he would continue with this same behavior. She admitted, "I just could not tolerate his disrespectful actions. I shut my eyes and pictured what it would be like to be married to this man, and what came out on the other side was not a good picture, so I walked away." Joy confirms "the one" did not end happily ever after.

Although Joy has experienced the joys of shopping for engagement rings, living with someone, and sharing her love, it all turned out to be disappointing. Joy confesses, "It's disappointing because it seems like it shouldn't be this hard. I feel like at this age, when I meet someone, I should not still be dealing with the same actions and behaviors as if I am still in my 20s." Joy strongly believes that men are often lazy when it comes to dating, and they shouldn't be. Men should be able to take the lead and put in the work, but they don't. Instead they see you, express interest, but expect the woman to take the reins and lead.

Joy is adamant that she is tired of people thinking something is wrong with her because her are single. "And it's even more frustrating when guy friends tell me that women have it hard because most of their male friends are dogs." Society has put a stigma on single women that something is wrong with them because they are single. "You are so intelligent, sharp, and beautiful, why are you single?" is a comment often heard by Joy. God has blessed Joy tremendously to be a strong and content woman in her current state of singleness. "I really believe that God has ordained everything in my life, and he's allowed me to be content with it. He has always put me in a space, whether good or bad, where he makes it ok, when he hears my cry. I have never been lonely for a man and I thank God for that. And after you have gone through so many challenges with guys, sometimes you are okay without those challenges of drama, and being by yourself."

But that doesn't steal the hope of one day being married from Joy. Joy has always wanted to get married; however, she never was the woman who set out to marry in her 20s or 30s. The greatest desire for Joy has always been having a solid relationship, a firm foundation, and then moving to the next step. And still today, she plays by those rules. Joy attributes her high self-esteem and her ability to love herself to the rearing of her mother. "My mom always said you don't need a man to do anything for you."

In this world of dating, Joy still doesn't feel rushed to be married; she has set standards for herself, and refuses to lower her standards just for the sake of having a man. "I know a lot of women who will settle just to say they have a husband; that's just not me. Society has changed so much, and now so many women are getting married later in life."

She eagerly awaits the day that she will marry, but she also knows that if God doesn't have a husband for her, she will be all right. She prays continually for a husband, and as she prays, she's not sitting idle, but instead has broadened her social network of dating prospects by joining Match.com. Match.com hasn't brought Joy any successful prospects as of today, but it's giving her a chance to meet people. She stays open in her options, especially when it comes to race. "Sometimes I feel as black women, we put all of our eggs into black men's baskets, causing us to lose out." Joy confides that she believes sometimes her honesty has been a turnoff for men, especially when it comes to sex. She shared with me how one guy in particular offered to give her a massage (and ladies, we all know what that generally means). In this instance, Joy responded to him no thank you, and then proceeded to tell him that men always offer her massages early on in conversations, which to her is an indication as to what they are expecting. After Joy shared her feelings with him, let's call him Ron, Ron proceeded to tell her, "I appreciate you expressing your feelings, however, I don't think I would like to continue this relationship of getting to know you. Good luck in finding the one!" So we all know what Ron's intentions were. Joy says it's situations like this that make it very difficult to date and want to get to know someone.

It's also challenging trying to keep sex out of the equation when you are dating, especially when you have gone there before. Because once you have gone there, you know what it feels like, what it's like, and it's hard to resist those temptations. Like so many single Christian women, including myself, it's easy to keep sex out of the equation and remain celibate as long as a man is not creeping around. I share Joy's sentiments; the hard part is trying to find a man who is willing to take the celibate journey with you as you two get to know each other. She admits that's when prayer comes into play. And you have to ask God to send someone into your life that is on the same page and has God's expectations for your life and the relationship. "I prayed this morning that while I go through this process of dating, that God will give me the strength to walk in the path that he would want me to walk when it comes to sex. I always pray for a man that will come into my life that will be on the same page that I am on when it comes to intimacy. That's a challenge, because when you tell a man that you are not going to have sex and he says ok, then in the back of your mind, you think he's with someone else."

In the meantime, Joy celebrates her singleness in the many things that she has accomplished. As a single woman, "I have the freedom to do whatever I want." And that freedom has allowed Joy to make big moves in her lifetime; relocating from her home state of California, and then a second time when she spent a few years working in South

Africa. "With a husband, I would have had to discuss those options before I could have said yes."

Being single has allowed Joy to purchase her own house. She shared with me that the ex-boyfriend Tony didn't believe that she could and would do it, and when she did, he was completely surprised. "He believed me buying a house was not a possibility, that I could not do it by myself." Joy is ecstatic about the purchase of her house; however, it is a physical challenge for her not having a handyman onsite. Without a husband around, Joy has to take care of the day-to-day maintenance on her house, and sometimes misses having that companionship, intimacy, and friendship that you can share and depend on.

"A man brings physical security. I always feel secure and protected when I am in a relationship." Joy reflects on a time when she experienced a home invasion and she had to chase the burglar out of her house. "If I had a husband, I would not have been the one chasing the burglar. I would have been calling 9-1-1 while my husband chased the intruder."

Joy is not different from other women. She has always longed to be a mother. "I've always wanted children, and if I never have a child, I'll be disappointed—not devastated." As other women, because of her beliefs, Joy never wanted to have children out of wedlock, and because of that, to this day she has not physically given birth. As Joy approached 40, she realized that she was not going to have a child, and since in the back of her mind she always wanted one, she has begun the process of becoming a foster mother in hopes of adoption. At 47, Joy hopes that she still has the physical energy to run, play, and raise a child. "It's been a long, slow process, and I have prayed long and hard about it, and right now I am just trying to be patient in this journey."

For the Single Sister, from Joy:

"As single women, we talk about what we go through. If someone would come to me for advice, I would be adamant about them staying true to themselves and loving themselves, and if you love yourself, you will demand someone to love you the way you should be loved."

I'm Single, So What? Joy's Journey to Spiritual Contenment.

ZENOBIA'S TRUE STORY

Three married couples, one roof, and major dysfunction marked the childhood of Zenobia. Raised in a family where her mother and one aunt were in physically abusive relationships, and her other aunt was married to an alcoholic and in a verbally abusive relationship, Zenobia witnessed three men, three women, and abuse. Her mother was a functional alcoholic that went to work every day and to the bar every night. So Zenobia spent much of her young life cooking, cleaning, and taking care of the home with her brothers and sisters. And not only that, the couple next door was also in a dysfunctional relationship, so this tainted Zenobia's view of marriage. Because of this, she has never wanted to marry. She even cut off a relationship with a guy she was dating who gave her the impression that he wanted marriage. "Screech, I cut it off," she confirmed.

Recently, she found herself dating someone she was very much interested in, but over time she had prayed about her relationship with him, and right away the Lord showed her in a couple of months that he was not right for her. He was a nice Christian guy, had a stable job, but the Lord said, "What does he do for you?" She had to be honest with herself and the Lord. "He doesn't do anything for me intellectually; he doesn't stimulate my mind."

Now, of course, friends tell her that she's just too picky and that she should lower her standards. When I asked, "What are your standards?" I didn't see how she could go much lower than the basic needs of food, shelter, and clothing. Zenobia wants a man that is Christian, stimulates her intellectually, has a job—doesn't have to be white collar, but has to pay his bills on time; in other words, have his business in order. "I don't need anyone that is going to bring my credit score down, suck my savings account dry." But as she shared about a friend's list, "I don't need a man who only has money." Zenobia has lowered her standards, and no longer has a height requirement. But she still holds onto the need for him to be willing to have an AIDS/HIV test, someone who doesn't smoke, and she contemplates on whether or not he can be a recovering addict. He has to demonstrate trustworthiness and be loyal. "It's hard being a single, intelligent woman and finding someone that can stimulate your mind!" I had to agree with Zenobia on that one.

Although Zenobia herself has never wanted to be married, she thinks now from a spiritual viewpoint and believes that as long as God is in it, and all secrets are on the table, including finances, debt, and open communication lines, then a marriage can work. Speaking spiritually, Zenobia confesses that she would marry now, but only if the Lord was leading her to that. "I allow the Lord to lead and guide me now because I follow him, but I think it would be a difficult decision, challenging for me, because I have been single for so long. But I think the Lord will help me through the obstacles."

Singleness is a part of who Zenobia is, because she's been doing it for 59 years. There are times when her singleness has stood out for her personally. She remembered looking at the wedding pictures from her son's wedding, noticing that the only unmarried people were her and her granddaughters; everyone else was with their significant other or spouse.

It's occasions like this that stand out for the single woman! Or in Zenobia's case, also not wanting to go to certain events alone. Zenobia is very cultured, and very much into sports and the arts. But who wants to go to a Cavs, Browns, or Cleveland State University game alone? How many single women want to go the theater alone? Not many. Like Zenobia, many of us will go to the museum or go to dinner by ourselves, but, "Sometimes you just want someone to go with you, like to the orchestra at Blossom Music Center," she shares. To clarify, Blossom is an outdoor arena where you can take lawn chairs, a blanket, a basket, and enjoy an outdoor concert. Who wants to do Blossom alone, or summertime festivals, or taking summer walks in quaint areas of the city alone? Hmmm, not many!

But don't get it twisted. Just because Zenobia doesn't want to do certain things by herself doesn't mean that she lacks any confidence. She is a self-confident and self-assured professional woman. "I have never lacked self-esteem! I just believe that everyone is not going to be married, and someone has to be single, and that is my lot in life."

Getting older helped Zenobia realize that she was probably going to be single the rest of her life, so she started studying singleness from a Christian perspective and learned how to accept being single. Zenobia admits that she has dated and would love to date or have a friend to spend time with, but she refuses to get sucked into the lifestyle that society tries to place on single women, like getting set up on blind dates, getting hooked up. Zenobia keeps herself out of situations where she stands solo as the only single person. "Stopping people from speaking negative to me about my singleness helps me to accept my singleness. I don't let people talk negative to me like that, because I am okay with it." She confidently said, "When someone says something about my being single, I check them, and those around get the hint and then no one else says anything else to me about being single."

In the same breath that Zenobia speaks candidly about her abstinence, she speaks honestly about her son being born when she was 17 years old, and her promiscuity in her 20s and 30s. But today,

Zenobia has been abstinent for close to 30 years. WOW! Single women, take heed that it is possible, and I know she has dated in those 30 years. To keep the devil at bay and from putting sexual thoughts in her mind, she stays clear of pornography, sexually illicit romance novels, television, and movies. "I don't read stuff that perpetuates immorality or fornication. I don't let my mind go there. I may look at a guy and say he's fine, but I don't daydream into a sexual state. I can control my thoughts; but that doesn't mean I don't have the urge." To combat those urges, Zenobia has found other outlets to keep the devil at bay, because "When you are doing nothing, the devil gets in your head." She jokes, "I even stay away from family, especially certain family gatherings, because I already know it's a hookup." Zenobia attributes her contentment in being single and able to handle desires to her relationship with Christ. Christ keeps her grounded and keeps temptations at bay. Christ comforts when it's a nice sunny Saturday afternoon and Zenobia is on her balcony reading a book "because my standards are so high." Her relationship with Christ keeps her focused on HIM instead of of being lonely, without a man, and sex.

Being single has afforded Zenobia the opportunity to actively work in her church. Singleness allows her to travel for work at the drop of a hat. "If the job calls and needs someone to go somewhere, then I can go. Being single has allowed me to volunteer for projects and has put me in a favorable position for work. The only thing I have to do is put my mail on hold," she laughs. Because she is single, Zenobia has had ample time to become very mature in the Word, because she has "unlimited quiet time." If she comes in the house, she doesn't have to clean, cook, wash clothes, or make up the bed if she doesn't want. If she wants, she can spend the entire evening in the bed with her Bible. Zenobia doesn't have to tend to anyone else but her relationship with the Lord. Now that's a benefit to being single.

But on the flip side, being single for Zenobia has sometimes been financially hard, and because she refuses to be a borrower, as the word of God tells in Proverbs 22:7, she sometimes falls financially short. Other times, Zenobia experiences a challenge in her singleness in not having someone to fix things around the house. "I am not a put-it-together kind of person, so if it says assembly required, I say never mind, or pay extra to have it assembled."

Dying alone is also a challenge for Zenobia. Because she is alone, she fears that if something happens to her, no one will find her for 4 or 5 days. "I have always thought about that. But God hasn't let anything happen to me."

For the Single Sister, from Zenobia:

"Embrace your singleness because it is a gift from God, because everyone can't live a single life. Everyone cannot thrive in that environment. There are a lot of married people that wish they were single because they think the grass is greener on the other side, but sometimes the other side is artificial turf. Embrace your singleness, because it's God's gift for your life. Someone has to be available to promote the kingdom of God. Married people are still required, but being single gives you a greater work into kingdom-building. Understand that it is what it is! Stick by Proverbs 18:22, "Whoso findeth a wife findeth a good thing, and obtaineth favour of the Lord." If it is God's will that you be married, that will happen. Don't try to put yourself in places where you might find someone. Focus on the Lord and let him hook you up instead of other people hooking you up or trying to set you up. I had someone tell me that sitting at home will not get me a husband. And my response was it can, a new UPS man may be on the delivery route or at the wrong house. But I'm not saying stay in the house, just don't be thirsty, throwing yourself at everyone. Focus on God because he knows who that one is, and he will bring him to you when you are ready for him."

I'm Single, So What? Zenobia's Journey to Spiritual Contentment.

TAMARA'S TRUE STORY

In her last year of college, she met a nice guy. They dated for months without sharing in sexual relations. She doesn't even remember them kissing. And then a few months before her college graduation, Tamara gave in to the sexual temptation of her tall, chocolate man. Two months before college graduation, at 23 years old, Tamara found herself pregnant with a son. Tamara and her boyfriend continued dating, even decided to move in together, and then two years later he proposed. She began planning for the wedding, but didn't get far. The wedding plans were put on halt because the relationship was not working. "Marriage was a bandage for the mistakes we had made. We were young and we did things out of order, not according to the will of God."

Tamara admits that oftentimes she deals with depression and sadness, because she wishes she had done things differently, done things God's way. "If I had done things the right way, God's way, I may still be in this situation, but I would be content because I would have done things in God's will, instead of thinking that it is because of the mistakes I made."

Tamara mourns the loss of wasted time, she wasted dating the wrong people. All because she was desperate for love, a relationship, and marriage, and more importantly, being outside the will of God. "If I was within the will of God, I would not have felt that desperation." Tamera reflects on a relationship in which she wasted five years of her dating life. In this particular man, she found no similarities except a strong attraction and a hope that he would one day change. That change never came, and instead she compromised her views on parenting, spirituality and marriage. "I compromised my values to be with this person. Someone I knew I did not need to be with, someone who did not value the things that I valued," she admitted.

Today, Tamara has found contentment because of her strong relationship with Christ, and she is seeking Christ and appreciating different qualities in a person. "Now that my relationship is strong with Christ, not that I did not know him before. But now I seek him and his will, and now someone's character is really important, when it seems that's something that should have been so important before but I overlooked it," she explained. Selfishly she admits that although she has a son, it would be nice to date someone without children because so often there is drama with "baby mamas," and in her current situation, her son's father is active in her son's life. They have learned to maintain a healthy relationship for the sake of their son. But while she waits on that "someone" she doesn't have to compromise her values for, she will continue to have fun getting to know new people, especially getting to know those people who have good character; people who have good values and love God. Tamara proudly shares with me, "I find contentment in those areas, getting to know other people and wanting it to turn into a relationship."

And some days more than others, Tamara wants that relationship to turn into marriage. But sometimes she wonders if it really will. She feels like she's missed the boat of actually finding someone she can spend the rest of her life with because she is older. At 42, with her eyes wide open, she now has formulated this list of requirements that she wants and expects in a mate. "Even with the guy that I am currently dating, I really like him, but it's hard for me to envision spending my life with him. When I was younger, I could see it. Now that I am older, I cannot see it. When you are younger you are more accepting to deficiencies, and more willing to work with different quirks. Now it's so hard to picture that fairy tale." And because of that disappointment, she sometimes finds herself self-sabotaging, like in her current situation. "I am waiting on something to happen, like finding something I don't like about him."

Discouragement causes Tamara to think that she may not be able to find someone; especially that someone that she wants to marry. At times Tamara used to wallow in her discouragement and fear. That fear of being disappointed because you are discouraged and already thinking negative about the outcome, instead of loving like you have never been hurt. Tamara admits that her discouragement, disappointment, and fear does not come from the fact that she does not have a husband, but it does come from regret. Regret that when she looks back, she wishes she could have done things differently; obediently. "Day to day I am cool with not having a husband, but when I think about the people I wasted time with, I have a lot of regret." She also admits that celibacy has been a struggle for her, which is important to her in her relationship with Christ. "It is hard trying to find someone that respects and understands it. It's easy being celibate when you are not dating someone that you are attracted to, or if you are not dating anyone at all. I know for some people, it's hard even when they are not dating anyone; they are still looking for sex. For me, it's only a problem when I'm dating someone. I am not going to go out and look for it, but when it's right there, it is hard. I find myself praying about celibacy all the time. Praying about it and trying to stay out of compromising situations, like going to someone's house," she admits.

Making decisions by herself and not having someone to bounce ideas off of plays a role in Tamara's frustration towards singleness. She explains that sometimes being single gets lonely; not always, but sometimes. The loneliness hit home when Tamara's son left for college. It was then that she realized she was single, because when he was home he was a distraction for her. When he left, she had to deal with the reality of being by herself.

But she is accepting and living content in her singleness. "I accepted my singleness by strengthening my relationship with God. I am more content because of Christ. He gives me peace even though I am single. I don't like being single, but Christ gives me the peace and contentment I need in my singleness. I don't try to manipulate situations or date people I am not supposed to."

Being single has allowed Tamara to purchase her own house, and raise a young, educated Christian man. Tamara can admit that sometimes she wonders that if God would have allowed her to have a husband, children, family, early, would she be as dependent on him as she is now, or would her focus have been on her family and she'd place God on the back burner. Sometimes God knows how to get our attention, and in her singleness and concentration on him, Tamera is active in her church, leads a ministry, volunteers for church conferences and seminars, and is a faithful tither.

For the Single Sister, from Tamara:

"Do not waste time with the wrong person, just because you need something to do. Do not lower your standards!"

I'm Single, So What? Tamara's Journey to Spiritual Contenment.

JEANETTE'S TRUE STORY

New York, New York, where dreams are made. Jazz, ballet, tap, modern dance, Alvin Ailey; it's Jeanette's turn to shine. After a number of courses in dance, a ballet teacher encouraged her to follow her dreams because she had the "it" factor; that it factor that dance instructors hope to find in all their students. That it factor that lead Jeanette to putting her law school desires on hold, even after taking the LSAT to pursue a dance career in New York.

Jeanette found her way to a summer program with the Alvin Ailey dance company and if she made it through, she would have the opportunity to dance and perform with the second company of Alvin Ailey. Despite her hard work, Jeanette didn't become a part of the second dance company, but she took additional classes through Alvin Ailey and returned to the Cleveland area to continue her career, finding herself engrossed in a number of great dance opportunities with The Cleveland Contemporary Dance Theater, the Cleveland Barons, trained with Michael Metcalf, and even made it to the last round of becoming a Cleveland Cavalier dancer. I teased her about being a Cleveland Cavs dancer, because after hearing her story, there was no way I could see her in the uniform of the dancers. She remarked, "God knew and I knew it wasn't going to work when I saw that they were doing a calendar in bikinis." Forthright and honest, Jeanette admits that she is happiest when she is either dancing or getting her praise on *"in all things being diligent and to the glory of God"*

(Acts 18:25). Years of wear and tear on her knees, and Jeanette knew it was time "to get a big girl job." And as a single woman with only a bachelor's degree, she secured a job as a high-level manager, which is typically unheard of in education.

After returning home from New York, she moved in with her mother until she got on her feet through substitute teaching, which ironically is when she realized how much she loves teaching. And because of that passion for teaching, she graduated with a master's degree in Spring 2014, and plans to pursue her PhD to enhance the lives of college students. For the first time in her life, she is proud of the fact that she is living on her own in a downtown apartment.

Single life isn't always easy for Jeanette, especially when it comes to celibacy and maintaining a 15-year on and off again relationship, with truly the only man she has ever loved. She lights up as she speaks of him. "It's something that I cannot put my finger on. I really like him. He is hilarious, really funny in the way that he makes you laugh about something years and years after it's happened. He's not slapstick funny; actually, he's introverted. But he'll have you falling all over the place laughing while he's just sitting there. He's got mad swag, and all these years later, I still feel some type of way. I still feel chills. He sees the world very differently, and in some ways that creates a lot of conflict, and in other ways it intrigues me about him."

Throughout their relationship, particularly with the off again time, he's dated other people and so has she. But the chemistry keeps bringing them back to each other, which makes it difficult for them to maintain celibacy. Losing her virginity to him after 8 or 9 months into the relationship, Jeanette dealt with a remorseful heart. She had given away something she couldn't get back, and given him something she couldn't share with anyone else, her virtue. She admits, "If I could do it over again, I would not have had sex the first time. And because sex means so much to me, it's hard to sever the relationship, because I am so connected to him, and it may have been different if I had never had sex."

She remembered a story her mother told her when she first left for college. "There are going to be a lot of temptations, and what happens is young people will make decisions contrary to what they know will be right, but just because you make that choice, doesn't mean you have to stay there, or that choice doesn't have to define who you are or who you become." And Jeanette has not let the decision to have sex early on in her relationship define who she is. "Even though I am not a virgin, I don't have to stay there. I may occasionally go too far, but I am not someone who has sex with anyone that is not my husband. But I am someone that battles with remaining holy and pure." Jeanette admits that at 35 it is tougher to remain celibate, because by nature she feels that she is a sexual person and knows what sexual desire feels like. To maintain her celibacy, she stays away from those desires that lead to sexual temptation, although sometimes she plays with fire.

Jeanette is a faith walker, and prays daily because of her desires. Jeanette admits, "I'm not always successful; it hasn't been intercourse again since the first time, but other things that are sinful in the eyes of God, and what you think in your heart that you are. Sin begins in the heart." Jeanette is a strong faith walker and I would discourage women from being in this situation because most are unable to handle the temptation. because most women could not handle that type of temptation; the rubbing, the touching, the petting. Losing her virginity was tough for her but she still maintains a few firsts to share with her husband, like having an orgasm.

Jeanette works hard to keep her thoughts pure and being willing to wait on God and do things his way, but of course it gets challenging. Like all of us, she shares, "Sometimes I feel as if I do this, I try to help him speed things up, not interfering with his plans." And I have already stated that the omniscient God does not need our help!

The chemistry that keeps Jeanette in this relationship also causes break-ups. It's this chemistry and the sexual desire that she has for him that has caused their break-ups, because he, like her, expresses his love and connection through touch and intimacy, while she maintains that her relationship and obedience with Christ is more important and says, "I don't want to fall outside of his will." And because Jeanette refuses to succumb to the temptations of intercourse, sometimes "he has to shut off a part of himself, but then it makes him not feel a connection towards me, and that's not good either, because he then doesn't treat me good. When he's connected, he treats me good." Like her, he can't deal with the disconnection so they break up. While broken up and not official , she found out he cheated on her. He knew she would not be happy because like everyone I know, who wants to share?

It was during those times that Jeanette also set a foundation for her expectations and the expectations of the relationship. At one point he had gotten back together with an ex-girlfriend. This was early on in the relationship, and he called Jeanette, but Jeanette refused to talk to him because she did not want to do to another woman what she didn't want done to her.

Jeanette is very understanding of her boyfriend's view on sex, but she sticks by her beliefs. "There is no way God is going to bless that, and I know it's hard for him to understand because he didn't see that type of religion." The religion where you went to church but you still tried to be sanctified in your sexual purity. And this foundation has led him to know that Jeanette is different; her faith, her belief, sets her apart. He's even commented that she is the best person he knows. And from the mouth of his mother, she's told Jeanette that he's said, "She's my soul mate."

And Jeanette is hoping to find that soul mate, someone she can spend the rest of her life with. Whether it is him or not, she's unsure, because they had been close once before, even attending pre-marital counseling. But the problem for Jeanette was that he could not set a date, he knew he wanted to marry her, but he couldn't say next week, next month, or next year, and that wasn't good enough for Jeanette. She needed more. She needed something concrete. So they agreed to end the relationship. This was not the expectation of Jeanette to go through pre-marital counseling classes to end in a break-up. She was devastated. She had never been so low in life and could not find a way to come back from it. "All I could do was keep my head up. I was really broken."

It was also a time when someone around her was either getting engaged, married, or having children. "All those things that I thought should happen to me were happening to someone else. They are all experiencing these joys and they are not doing it God's way. And here I am, trying to do it God's way, but they are getting the joys. Why are they getting it and I'm not?"

It was nothing but the grace of God that brought Jeanette back. "If it had not been for the grace of God, where would I be?" One thing that Jeanette has always had when times have gotten hard is the grace of God. "I always lean on God. I go to my hymns, my scriptures, my best friend and my mom; people who speak life into me." It's also the grace of God that helps Jeanette get through the struggles of being single, like frustration, discouragement, loneliness, and anxiety. Jeanette divulges, "There are moments when I feel very anxious and want it to happen now, so I can have sex now and we can move on with our lives. Or there are moments that I feel discouraged because there are times when he hasn't done or I think he should have done something, and then I think it's not going to happen." Bridal showers, bouquet tosses, and Beyoncé's "Single Ladies" are constant reminders to Jeanette that she is still single. Jeanette fesses up, "I'm getting at that point now where I'm asking, is it going to be possible for me to have children if I don't marry the person I'm with now?" Like a number of Christian single women, it's challenging not wanting to choose your carnal desires/needs when you feel like he is the love of your life and you need him. But Jeanette says it best, "I need God more."

As a single mom and a self-witness, Jeanette's mom speaks life into her by living as an example of self-sacrifice. Her mom sacrificed a relationship, love interest, to teach her daughter that you can survive being a Christian single woman without sex if you do it God's way. "I learned how to enjoy the other things God places in life. God will be your sufficiency, he will make you content. He will never let you down. You may have moments of sorrows, even months, years, but he will give you the assurance. I am okay with God and I dig me, I like me."

"A huge sense of pride for me is that I know God, and have a relationship with him and that he's kept me," she proudly confirms.

For the Single Sister, from Jeanette:

"Stop believing that you are not going to find anyone if you don't have sex. And don't put yourself in the predicament, don't let him give you a massage, because once they get accustomed, it's hard not to desire them that way and them not to desire you that way. Do it God's way and you will spare yourself unnecessary heartache. There will be heartache. Tribulations are certain. We are going to have hardships but you will spare yourself unnecessary hardships and consequences if you just wait on God, because he is faithful. I don't have it all figured out, I am a work in progress, but I do mean to go right on until the battle is won."

I'm Single, So What? Jeanette's Journey to Spiritual Contentment.

MARIE'S TRUE STORY

Madonna sang "Like a Virgin, touched for the very first time." Like a virgin? Nope, Marie is a virgin, and when God blesses her with a husband, she will have been touched for the very first time. In a world filled with sexual immorality, lust, and promiscuity, Marie has maintained her virtue for over 38 years. "It's not easy. If I were not a Christian and wanted to have a one-night stand, then I would go for it. But I know that's not what HE's calling me to do, so I have to wait for it. There are plenty of times that I want to have sex with that man, right there, but then I come back to sanity. When I like a guy I start praying, Lord help me."

Of course, Marie thought she'd be married by this age. "I'm going to do this, graduate from high school, go to college by this time, and have my first child by this time. Had my whole life mapped out—but now I'm re-working the plan. Some things are just not the way I thought they would be." It's obvious that Marie's desire to live a holy life and her relationship with Christ has enabled her to live in a state of contentment. "I really like my life, so it's not a sense of urgency that I have to get out of this state. It's not like being in prison and I have to get out of here. It's more like I'm at a resort and I'm asking myself how can I extend my stay."

Marie would like to be married and she says, "I will love that life, but I am not going to hate my life because I am single. Whatever state I am in, I am content. I am having a great time." She ties her being single into an analogy of how God loves us. When God looks at taking care of us, he looks at our whole life. Unlike God, when we look, we look at right now and we see right now, because that's what our flesh tells us. But when God looks, he sees it all. It's important to step out and look at things the way God sees them. "I want to be married, but it's important for me not to put myself in a situation where I am not going to please God. He does not want me to sleep with someone I am not going to marry. Someone who has not put a ring on my finger. Live with someone I am not married to. God doesn't want that. When he says we can trust him, I know I can. I just work with the things that I have in being content."

Marie loves the right now. The right now car, the right now house, the right now state she's in. However God wants to use her, she is willing to let God use her, whether as a resource for her family and/or her community. She is going to do what God wants her to do.

Like many of us, Marie wants to spend her life with someone. She believes there is a whole other part of her that would come alive if she were to marry. It would be like unleashing and developing a talent that you discovered. Marie believes that God has a husband for her, but if not, she knows that it is his will and she is still going to have joy and enjoy every adventure.

In the meantime, there are so many things that occupy Marie's mind and allow her not to focus on what she doesn't have or what she isn't doing. She is blessed to spend time with nieces, nephews, family, and friends. She was leaving our interview to go and bake a cake for her niece. "If I don't have children it would be okay, because I have good people I can pour my money into and they are waiting. If I can help you, then I am glad." And because of this generosity, Marie has been blessed to buy a house at a young age, and travel. She has taken multiple road trips with friends and family. She shared an experience with me in which she and her friends took a cross-country trip from

Ohio to Virginia Beach, to Georgia, Florida, Louisiana, Texas, and then drove to the Grand Canyon, Vegas, Denver, and Kansas. Friends and family flew in and out to meet up with Marie and travel from one state to the next. Her theme for travel is "Planes, trains, and automobiles." When summer hits, she doesn't mind hopping in her car and driving.

Marie is also thankful for the wonderful friends she's had since college that still get together for holidays and special events. She has the support of great family, who have been there through the good, the toils, and the heartaches. And some of those heartaches include the loss of her mother, stress at work, gaining 20 pounds, struggling with self-esteem . . . but those heartaches, according to Marie, didn't come from the challenges of being single. Instead they came from just living life. "It doesn't matter whether you are married or single. You are going to have to work through problems. Deal with loss and deal with grief." But there are some things that she admits might be a little easier if she were married, having someone to take her car to the shop, a plus one at events, and companionship. It would be nice for Marie to have teamwork, the value of doing something together. "Makes life richer when you are sharing your life."

Marie is focused, and because of that, she has been able to counter and challenge a lot of the obstacles that occur with being single. Unlike some women, it's easy for Marie not to be in a relationship because it's hard for her to allow someone into her space. She admits that she meets men all the time; that's how I found out how much she loves riding bikes, when she shared a dating story. Marie met a guy who called and asked her out. She agreed and he offered to pick her up. As he arrived, she watched him from her window chain his bike to a tree. Needless to say, Marie ended up being the driver of this date. Because of his failure to share his love of bike riding, the first date was very awkward. Well, like many of my own dating experiences,

Marie's didn't start good, progress good, or end good. Marie and I laughed as we share details of being magnets for older men.

For Marie, marriage is more than just saying she has someone. She wants to be in a fulfilling relationship. It's unbelievable for her to hear how many men won't accept "No", when she refuses to give her number; she knows they are only looking to have a good time. "I don't care that I won't have a date with someone tomorrow who is drunk today." Marie explains why she would not want to date someone who introduces himself tore up with alcohol; that's not impressive to her. That is a turnoff.

She verifies, "I am not going to do things that aren't good for me." She remembered meeting a guy out of town who was only interested in having a one-night stand. And she admits even though she may have wanted to, why would she, when he didn't want to know anything about her? Marie knows that she cannot hold onto a man just because of sex. "Nothing is that magical that it is going to keep a guy. If he is going to marry me, he will."

Marie was meeting man after man, and it had gotten to a point where she realized, "I don' t like any of you, and if I don't like you, why would I want to be near you? And so I would pull back."

I had to ask, was there anyone that she ever thought about losing her virginity to? She explained, there were men she liked and wanted to go further with, but losing her virginity is a big deal. And since she wasn't madly in love with them, she just couldn't bring herself to go there. She never wanted to cross those boundaries with someone she was not in love with. I applaud Marie for her commitment to God and maintaining her celibacy.

There was one particular guy that Marie dated in which those boundaries became scary. "There was a guy I liked, but we were not on the same page. I knew if I felt this way about him now, if we had sex, it would be over. This guy was going to fry my brains." Marie started praying immediately for God to show her who he was and if he was not for her, to then get him out of her life. Don't pray for God to remove someone from your life or to show you their true colors unless your heart is open to receive the information from God. Because Marie is in constant prayer and has a strong relationship with Christ, her heart was open to hear the will of God. Because Marie kept sex out of the situation, she could clearly see that this guy's behavior was opposite of what she stood for. He was a heavy drinker, smoker, and swearer. He was even financially irresponsible. But the ultimate was when he told her he didn't think Jesus was the only way you can be saved. She retaliated, "What if we have a kid, and the school says where is his dad, and I say I don't know, when we both know you are the father. It is the same with the Lord." In other words, if your child denies you as his father, think how you would feel. Well, that is the same way God feels when you deny Christ as his son.

They had a lot of chemistry, that could have made Marie lose her virginity, because he was charismatic, honest, and funny. He was even more honest than she was, she admits. It was the same honesty that led to hurt and the relationship not working. "I wouldn't want to jeopardize my house because I want a new pair of shoes. I wouldn't sacrifice my entire life with God for this one thing. If it's right, then let's works on it. Otherwise, let's just go our separate ways. I don't want to be connected to someone because sex has power over you and I don't want anyone to have that power over me. I have to be able to trust someone."

Today, Marie admits that she is more upfront with guys about her choice not to engage in premarital sex. At this age, Marie is like a number of single women; her network for dating has decreased. She doesn't go out much; she's tried e-harmony, but got tired of all the questions. She admits she never got into a routine where she could be successful with online dating. Being alone affords her the opportunity to not buy groceries if she doesn't want to, and not to have to change the thermostat to accommodate someone else's needs. "When you share your life you share their mess, and that's what I don't like." How many of us as single women really want to share in someone else's mess? Not me!

I get a big kick out of hearing Marie talk about God's plan for the family when she clearly struggles. "This whole plan that God has for the family doesn't work for me. Like being submissive, because I can't submit to an idiot. Clearly I know the answer to the question; if I had been a man, everything would be perfect. I don't trust easy. I have always put myself in a position of power. If we are going someplace, I have my own ride and my own money. I always felt like I want to take care of myself. It works so much better when the plan comes from me and then they follow it," she laughs heartily. But she admits that the flipside of that is not good. "If God gives him to me, then I have to pull back. So I think it's going to matter who I marry. If I am going to make God happy, me happy, and this man happy, it has to be a perfect fit." Marie knows that she needs a man that is strong, assertive, and confident and can hold a conversation. "It makes me nervous when I am around people who don't have anything to say." She's working on her submissiveness; she's learned to be cooperative, and it's becoming easier to submit to others that can make sound decisions.

Marie spends her days focused on her students. "I love being a teacher. I believe it's my calling." Teaching allows Marie to build up the community while making a living. She has been blessed to receive accolades as a teacher. She has been put in a position to help other teachers become better teachers. She is nationally board certified. She has her master's degree. She's been teacher of the year and Black School Educator of the year.

For the Single Sister, from Marie:

"In the words of Al Green, everything is going to be alright." Marie wanted to share with the Single Sister words that she received from a singles event she once attended. Hole, Whole, and Holy—There are people who are suffering from holes because everything they take in is seeping out, and the holy way to fill those holes is with Christ. And once he fills those holes, then he can fill us up and we can be fulfilled. We must live Whole to feel complete, not watching for someone else to come into our lives. Work on us, put yourself in the community, and help your family. We must also live Holy-Spiritual and whatever God has planned for you, you are going to get it."

I'm Single, So What? Marie's Journey to Spiritual Contenment.

ESTHER'S TRUE STORY

Her eyes began to water. "A lot of times when I am lonely, Jesus is my best friend! My life doesn't depend on waiting on this ultimate husband because I have learned to be content with him. Jesus is my main squeeze! I know him, and I can communicate with him. When we get together in a room, it's explosive."

Married at 21, Esther was divorced six years later. What started as a fantasy of a white picket fence, the husband, the children, all turned wrong after the honeymoon. Esther was blind to any signs that this was not the man for her, because she had formed in her mind and had emotionally been overcome by what she expected the marriage to be instead of what the marriage was. Although she stayed with her ex-husband for six years, Esther admits that there was a strain on the marriage the first two or three months after the honeymoon. There were a lot of peaks and valleys in the relationship; more valleys than peaks. But it was a learning experience for Esther. It has turned her into the God-fearing woman she is today.

Esther happily admits, "Sometimes I felt like the Lord allowed me to go through it so that he could present the blessing that he had for me; because through all of that I had a blessing, a life-changing blessing." Esther sprouted from that experience. She admits that she made a mistake by not following God's plan and because of that, there were consequences. She even wonders how she made a mistake in choosing a husband, when she had been raised to know the value of marriage and had been taught her whole life what the biblical roles of a husband and wife should be. But Esther chose who she thought she should marry; who she thought was the one. "God says in his word, *he that finds a wife finds a good thing (New American Standard Version*, Proverbs 18:22), I found him.

The next man I marry, the Lord will have to slap me and say, this is the one. If the Lord says the same, then I would get married again," she smirked. "I really believe that, because I know I am not moving until God tells me. As good as he looks, as sweet as he may be, if he is not the one, I am not moving. It's me and him every morning. I say Lord, you lead the way. And when he leads, a hectic day isn't bad because he's in it," she proclaims of Jesus Christ.

Esther dates occasionally, but she still has a slight fear of not wanting to be hurt again. Her sisters and friends tease her because she is oblivious as to when a man is interested in her. Single women, we have got to become more aware of our presence. God has created beauty in all women, and single women, there is someone that recognizes it. "When a guy is flirting with me, I am so used to blowing it off that it takes a friend or sister to say he likes you." But flirting is not Esther's main focus. After quickly commenting on dating, she turns her attention back to Jesus. "I am happy with Jesus, and I do not want anyone to mess that up."

Esther's failed marriage has taught her that when she leaves God out, "it's dangerous" to her. As a young adult in her third year of college, her dad begged her not to marry her ex-husband and to finish school first, but Esther did not want to miss the opportunity to be married. She "did not want to miss the boat." Of course with maturity and age, Esther cannot believe that today she is the person at 21 that did not want an opportunity to be married. No longer is Esther bothered by the pressures of being single. No longer does she worry that others see her as a failure because her marriage did not work, because she knows that God had a plan for her life. "From pre-teen years to becoming a young woman, women are taught that they have to have a man, or they have to be in a relationship to be successful. I'm here to tell you—that is far from the truth in order to feel self-worth," she proudly proclaimed.

Singleness for Esther allows her to be more available to God for service. She spends her time helping her parents, her sisters, her church, and the community. Even her job is ingrained in a mission of helping others. Esther is proud that God affords her the chance to help others. "I really believe that the Lord brought me home after my marriage because I was a help to so many," she confesses, and then she explains that God had a purpose for her. "I want you to understand that you are here so I can use you." When we allow God to use us for his purpose, our work is never in vain, and our discomfort of what brought us to this point becomes comfortable in knowing that God directed it.

Esther's state of singleness allowed God to expose her God-given gifts and talents, such as serving as an effective leader in her church. Esther has been able to use God-sanctioned visions to carry out HIS work through the mission of his ministry. Understand that Esther doesn't claim to prophesy or speak the future, but what she does confirm is that God has blessed her to work visions and plans for his glory in her current church leadership role. When God gives Esther a vision for a new program or a new idea, he puts all the pieces to the puzzle in place so that he can be glorified. God is constantly giving her things to share with those that are willing, with those that are skeptical, and even those who are inquisitive. And in spite of people's personal goals, God allows HIS plan to move forward.

Esther is proud that "being single has helped me to know what my gifts are and to use them without any hesitation." Esther uses her gifts because she believes God will take away gifts that are not used.

Because Esther is single, she is much more available than the average woman in a relationship because she doesn't have to give her time to children or a husband. "It's just me and Jesus, and it benefits everyone around me." Being single can sometimes become overwhelming for Esther, just as I heard from so many women, including myself, because so many people want so much. When you are single, people believe that you have oh so much time on your hands to do whatever they want. But sometimes as single women, we cannot do everything for everybody. Esther said it plainly, "The same people who tell you that you look tired are the same people that will ask you to do something."

But for Esther, things are changing. She is learning to allot time for herself. "I'm learning this year, and I'm taking baby steps in having more time for me." She is learning to juggle her time between herself and helping others. The same generosity that helps others is also the same generosity that hurts us, if we do not manage our "me time" well. Esther has made a promise that this year is a year of the "no." But she plans to make her nos a little more diplomatic. "I don't see that happening in my plans this year. I can't see myself doing that this year." You can't get more diplomatic than that.

Esther admits that sometimes it does get lonely, but those are the times when Jesus picks her up and cradles her in his arms. For Esther, it doesn't get as lonely as it used to right after the divorce, but having no one physically there to share her innermost thoughts with was the set-up for her to become dependent and acknowledge Jesus. She admits that her attention and focus needed to be on him. "I was never the type of person who has to be around people, so once I started studying God's word and looking at it more and talking to him, the loneliness subsided." Esther thought for a minute and laughed, "I don't even consider myself single," because she doesn't think about it much.

For Esther, being single came naturally; it was something she just did. After the divorce, she stopped thinking about it and let it go. Even when I asked her about doing the interview, she said she was like, "Hmmm, I guess I am single."

Jesus has also cradled her and helped her to accept that she is not a mother biologically, but she is a surrogate mother for so many nieces, nephews, church members, and community members. "I always ask the Lord why I didn't have children, because I believe I would be a good mother. I wanted to know what it felt like to carry a child for nine months." She smiled. Of course all mothers tell her, "No you don't!" Although Esther never considered adoption, she did take pride in the relationship she fostered when she found out her ex-husband, then-husband, had a child with another woman. I even wonder why God didn't allow Esther to have children, because her mothering instincts and her love for children exudes in her being. Esther promises, "I just will continue to be a trellis that other young people can grow on."

And she does have a thorn of regret knowing that marriage kept her from finishing school, but that regret will not last much longer, because at 52 years old, Esther is headed back to school this fall to get her Bachelor's Degree in Social Work. Growing up wanting to be either a social worker or teacher, Esther chose social work. She was always around social workers and witnessed how hard they work to help others. She plans on being "the ultimate social worker."

Esther hit me with this quote and at first I am puzzled, but then I began to listen and understand. "The steps of a good man are ordered by the Lord, but the steps of a good woman are ordered by the Lord." Then Esther begins to explain, "There is a reason we have steps, because steps allow the Lord to lead us one step at a time. We can't race up the steps." Esther remembers that when she was younger she used to race up the steps, skipping two or three steps at a time, but now she has to take each step one at a time for a reason, because "when you miss a step you stumble and fall, but if you take one step at a time, you learn a lesson from each one. The Lord has designed it that way because when you learn the lesson, then you can receive the blessing. I have to take one step at a time because when I skip one, God is going to take the situation or person to take me back to the step I missed to learn the lesson. As single women, we have to take one step at a time." Single women, are you taking one step at a time?

For the Single Sister, from Esther:

"Being single is not a bad thing. It is a blessing, and you need to find out what the blessing is. For single Christian women, get real close to the Lord, because he is going to be the one to reveal the lifestyle of being single and let you know that it is going to be okay. Single women, just relax. It is not your job to look; when that man comes, the Lord will let you know. The Lord is not about confusion, you will know. And if you do not know Jesus, then make a connection quick, because you are in double jeopardy being single and not knowing the Lord."

I'm Single, So What? Esther's Journey to Spiritual Contenment.

MS. JAY'S TRUE STORY

If she were given a second chance, she would marry him again. Ms. Jay spent 12 years of her marriage caring for her now deceased husband, and during their last year together, they continued to share in the magical moments that they had shared for so many years prior. Ms. Jay reflects on a time when she was by her husband's side during his hospital stay, and instinct would have it that she would reach out and place the palm of her hand on his, and instantaneously a sensation of warmth filled her body. For 33 years they shared a bond that didn't develop overnight, a bond that first was established through a friendship in 7th grade. Their relationship was an intimate relationship, a relationship filled with catering, pampering, caring, and love. A relationship with a great sex life! "We were like a foot in a hose, a hand in a glove." She couldn't stop smiling, thinking about their sex life.

At 62 years old, Ms. Jay has spent the last four years adjusting to life without her husband. A man who one day asked after so many years of friendship, "Why don't we just hook up?" She didn't resist, and the rest of the story is history because she proudly proclaims that he was her buddy, her friend. They began dating each other, and eventually the relationship led to marriage. She remarks that she believes he got in so good because he courted her son from a previous relationship first. And from that her son, as well as her father, grew very fond of her soon to be husband. At 27 years old, she knew she was ready to be married. Ms. Jay had been on her own since she was 17 and had dated a few here and there, but by that time she knew she wanted to settle down. She confesses that she presented the idea of marriage to him and he didn't reject it.

But after her husband's battle with cancer, Ms. Jay was left to hold the pieces together. She attributes God to being the glue that holds it together. When she was married, she never had to be responsible for home repairs, cutting grass, or paying bills. "I didn't have to live off my money, I lived off his," she proudly stated. Her responsibilities included cooking and assisting in raising her grandson. "I liked cooking for him, I just didn't like cooking so late. But since I don't cook late and as much, I have lost weight." She spent her life enjoying her husband and the time they shared, like traveling two or three times a year, getting excited about what sports teams were in the playoffs or Super Bowl. "My husband made such a big deal about the Super Bowl that I miss him more around then instead of his birthday," she laughs.

Marry again? That's not in Ms. Jay's immediate plans. She's not really dating, because as a number of women confess, there is nothing out there. Ms. Jay hasn't really talked to anyone in depth, but she has gone out with one or two guys. She admits that it's going to be hard to find someone that would pamper her like her husband did. She found herself excited about one potential man until he confessed to her that he was sick. It was a dream come true; he showed up with peach roses and chocolate-covered strawberries, two of her favorites, on his own merits, without any prompts from Ms. Jay. (If only someone would show up at my door without a prompt.)

Well, back to Ms. Jay. They went out a couple of times, until he told her he was on dialysis, and there are a few things that Ms. Jay knows the severity of and how much care goes into it, and that's kidney disease, chemical dependency, and drug addiction. "He was looking for a woman to step into his life and take care of him. He also did not realize the severity of his illness. And although I never minded taking care of my husband, I didn't want to do that for another man I'd just met, so I didn't even allow myself to go there." Ms. Jay went out with him one more time but in the meantime he had fallen and hurt himself, so that led to thoughts of, "Oh no, I don't want to take care of anyone!" In the midst of it all, Ms. Jay realized that she was getting older, and would probably wind up staying single because she eludes confidence and validates that she does not need a man.

But like most women, she admits that every now and again, it would be nice to have a companion. "I wish I had a list like when I was younger, a male friend or two that you could go out with and it didn't mean sex." And seeing as how Ms. Jay misses the sex with her husband, she's found herself falling into the trap of just sex, but she is looking for much more and she confesses, "I am too old to just sex." She is not willing to fall in love with someone and they not love her back, because the love she had with her husband is irreplaceable. She confesses that the desire for God to remove sex is on her prayer list, but admits that sometimes she's like, "Hmm, yes, put it on the list and then no, I don't want it on the list." We both agreed that the truth shall set you free, and God knows the purity of our hearts and our prayer request.

Right now Ms. Jay is just trying to grow in grace and not live life likes she's 20, but not acting like life is over. "I've done a couple of things by myself, but having someone to go to a play or do something with would be nice," she shares.

She's still learning to accept the fact that she is single; that's something she is working on. Even after the doctors had told her that her husband didn't have long to live, it took him being gone and her on the other side for reality to sink in, that it's just her and God, "because me and my husband did a lot of things together." But now as a single woman, she has time and she's trying to figure out what to do with the time. "If I was younger, I would have gone back to school. But now that I am older, I have to find something to do with my time," she said, puzzled.

Ms. Jay admits that if her husband was still alive she would have retired by now, but with him being deceased, she maintains that she is not quitting her job anytime soon or getting rid of her car. And yes, it's a nice car. She also knows that she enjoys living in her house with a huge basement. I could sense her getting emotional as she began to reflect on her blessings.

About a year after her husband's death, Ms. Jay remembers vividly sitting staring at bills, thinking and crying how was she going to make it. And God spoke, "Ms. Jay, you are still in the same spot you were at his death. I am the Provider; I used him to bless you. All you need to know is that I am going to do it again. You are going to be all right. I am the Provider." The comfort in God's voice allowed her to wipe those tears, put her makeup on, and allow God to continue providing.

Today, Ms. Jay continues to manage and maintain the lifestyle she had with her husband. She praises, "God in his awesomeness; my lifestyle hasn't changed that much." Although it gets challenging sometimes when, "I have to make major decisions, because we made most of our decisions together." Ms. Jay knows that, "God has been all right" with her and that she is just trying to stay pleasant and not walk around looking sad and pitiful. "My biggest peace right now is that I believe God feels that I need all this time for me. I feel that my life has become selfish taking care of me to show others that it's okay to take care of you, and I believe that it is my responsibility to take care of me. And to represent that life is okay on this side of the road," she smiles.

God had a plan for Ms. Jay, a plan that she confesses she would not have been able to devote time to had she been married. She serves as a project manager for community outreach. And she knows that if she had been married, time would not have allotted her the opportunity to work in a God-directed, God-sent position and assist so many people at zero cost to her program.

I noticed her eyes beginning to water as she shared a quick story. "God sent this to me, and this is where God said, you know I got you. From the first person who offered to help. I remember he said that his mother had told him that I needed some assistance and when he came to see me, he said 'God sent me to help you.' Can't nobody beat me talking about the God I serve, and God sent him to me to get things started because I didn't know where to begin. And from there God just sent people left and right, that offered this and that." In God's greatness a $300,000 program is functioning at zero cost. She is proud of her accomplishment. "I am just trying to make sure that the things God has entrusted me with, he gets the glory from. I am letting people know that God changes lives every day."

For the Single Sister, from Ms. Jay:

"Take good care of yourself and be mindful of your spending. I spend, but I'm being more mindful. It's hard to pay yourself first, but have something at the end of the year, have a couple of dollars set aside. You have to take care of you. You can't help me love me, because I don't have a problem loving me. God wants us to let people know that we love ourselves, so that people know that God lives in us. Sometimes you have to look in the mirror and have a good self-talk and remind yourself that you are responsible for taking care of yourself and no one can love you better than you, other than God."

I'm Single, So What? Ms. Jay's Journey to Spiritual Contenment.

Conclusion

There were many commonalities between the women interviewed from the challenges they face in being single to the thorns that affect their everyday state of contentment (fear, regret, time, loneliness, anxiousness, finances, sex, self-esteem, growing old, depression, discouragement). In Part One, I discussed a few of the thorns that affect women in their state of contentment. But as I interviewed these women I heard reoccurring themes with the challenges and thorns that affect women in their season of singleness. And a number of the challenges revolve around three specific areas: relationships, sex, and finances.

RELATIONSHIPS

I know oftentimes we don't like to admit that we seek companionship when we are single, because then it appears that we are desperate for a man. This is not desperation, this is human nature. People thrive on relationships. God created us to be in relationship with each other. God created Adam, but he then created Eve as a helpmate to Adam, a relationship. Abraham and Sarah, Rebecca and Isaac, Ruth and Boaz, had a relationship. David and Bathsheba had a relationship— not a healthy start, but they had a relationship. Now I could go on and on about the relationship that should exist between man and woman. I will not dwell on that. But what I will touch on is this idea of companionship, and and how it is not wrong to want companionship or to spend time with someone of the opposite sex.

Just recently, I decided not to attend an event because I was tired of going alone or going with female friends of mine. I wanted an escort, and not just any escort, but someone that I could enjoy an evening with. And this is where the problem lies. So often as single women, we get caught up in the idea of companionship that we either accept qualities below those we really want, or our demand is so high that we can't enjoy the company of just a friend. Relationships between men and women are tricky; we deal with different emotions as to why we are in or seeking relationships. Sometimes as women we experience loneliness, which in turn leads to making bad decisions in relationships. For instance, as single women, we may have the tendency to allow the emotion of loneliness to overpower our decision-making process and we put ourselves into relationships that are not good for our own well-being.

Fear also leads to us being dishonest in relationships for the protection of being hurt. In the past, as women, we have been hurt and disappointed so many times that when the door opens for someone new, we quickly shut ourselves off to avoid the possibility of being hurt again. We put up walls by not asking the right questions; and as a single woman, you have to define your right questions for your right needs. But questions like, are you a Christian; do you want to be married; have children? Do you have children? Are you bi-sexual, gay, and straight, on the down-low? Not being transparent or honest can lead to some difficult times and some hard times. Men are straightforward creatures, from-the-hip shooters. But as women, because we have a tendency to deal more in emotion or with our hearts instead of our minds, we tend to hold back pertinent information that can lead us to making decisions that are best for us.

Woman X dated a man for years not knowing that this man had

another life in another city. Don't ignore the signs, and do ask the questions.

Many times we will hear that the best place to meet a companion is at church. Most of us know that church does not have the perfect person, but hopefully someone striving to have the characteristics of Christ. But relationships in the church can be quite dangerous and quite good. How often do we walk in the doors of the church house to notice the women outnumber the men? In cases and scenarios of the sort, as single women, we risk the dangers of running into the man that can have multiple women in the same close quarters because we allow it (this does not only happen in the church exclusively).

Women, we have got to start holding men accountable for their actions. And on the flip side, women, we must take a man at face value. What a man typically says is what he means. We must also establish boundaries in relationships. Is he a plutonic friend? A friend with benefits? A friend on the road to exclusivity? A friend on the road to marriage? What is this relationship? Unlike women (and I know there are women who disagree that they are strong, independent daters), it is sometimes very easy for a man to date multiple women at a time (the weed-out process). Unlike women; when we meet a man, we are ready to be in an exclusive relationship off the bat.

Because it's human nature to be in relationship with another, there can be a tendency to formulate a non-existent relationship after only a few dates or just after a hello. Women, stop mistaking flirting for this man wanting a relationship. Most people who flirt, because they have nothing else to do; and I know that is the grounds for trouble, but it's true. Nine times out of ten, we flirt to see if we still got it, but we really don't want it.

I am not going to leave the men out in this brief segment on relationships because so often I hear from men, "Women are crazy," and my question is, "What did you do to make them crazy?" A man's behavior can be the driving force to the craziness of women. Reality check, men: a woman can be emotionally and mentally damaged by the actions of a man, just as a man can be emotionally and mentally damaged by a woman.

As Christian men and women who are seeking relationships, we have to make sure that we are in a healthy place to be in a prosperous relationship. We also must seek Godly advice in choosing mates and in just dating. Relationships are natural, but we must seek the Creator of human relationships in order to find a healthy companionship. Stop relying on self, and stop being inhibited by thorns of fear, hurt, loneliness, and disappointment that lead to unhealthy relationships.

SEX

Sex, sex, sex. In the '70s, Marvin Gaye graced the music scene with "Sexual Healing." In the '90s, Color Me Bad sang "I want to sex you up." Sex on the radio, sex on the TV, sex on the computer, sex in your house. Sex is everywhere, and if we go with everywhere, everywhere sex is justified and cool. As Christian women, we have been taught that premarital sex is against the will and command of God. *"Flee fornication. Every sin that a man doeth is without the body; but he that committeth fornication sinneth against his own body" (King James Version,* I Corinthians 6:18). I have heard conflicting testimony to this passage, and the practical theology and application in which Paul answers a series of questions asked by the church of Corinth. I write these conflicting views without revealing the sources of the information or statements. In conversations, I have discovered from men and women I would consider scholars of the Word and grounded in their spiritual beliefs to argue that in this passage of Scripture, Paul is writing to a particular church or group of people for a particular time period, so we must loosely base our practices on the passage's outline. In other words, premarital sex is ok.

I have been privy to hearing that as long as you are in a relationship that is ultimately leading to marriage, then premarital sex is cool. I have also had my ears open to; it is generally okay to engage in premarital sex as long as you are not out of control with it. In all of these conversations, my conviction has not changed; the Holy Spirit has not dealt with me differently. In these conversations, my conviction still remains that premarital sex is in contradiction to God's plan for man and woman, marriage. Now of course, I could go through a justification process and convince myself that premarital sex is ok, but I have to stick with my Godly convictions in my stance on premarital sex. And with that being said, I say to other women, you have to stand behind your own personal convictions. You also have to read and research for yourself so that you will know why you believe what you do.

In so many other books and reading material, we have heard that an exchange of sex equals an exchange of spirits, leaving behind a piece of you with each person you sexually engage with. This idea, along with fleeing fornication because of your relationship with Christ, is a no-brainer for some women. For others, it's a difficult task as I learned in conducting the interviews with other women, including myself. Abstaining from premarital sex is easy if I'm not dating. But how do we avoid something that is so good and so right for human relationship when you've already gone there? Awhh, that's the question. If you've never said yes, then you just don't know.

But what about those women who have had an active sex life and are then convicted to avoid premarital sex and practice a life of celibacy until God sends a mate? How does this woman date? She doesn't. Just kidding; no, as a Christian woman, dating without sex is a hard task, because how many men do you meet that refuse to date a woman because she maintains her celibacy and they can't handle it? How many times have we heard, "If he is not getting it from you, he's getting it from someone?" Is this true? Quite honestly, I don't know. I would pray that there are some men in this world that can respect a woman's choice to remain celibate or a virgin until marriage, just as I hope some women can maintain an honest, trustworthy relationship with a man who wants to remain celibate.

I remember speaking with a close friend who refused to date a woman because she was celibate. At first I was hard on him about the choice, but in the end I had to respect his honesty. He knew that he could not be in a relationship that was void of sex, so he didn't lead her on, he let her go.

I don't have all the answers for avoiding premarital sex, but I do have suggestions on how to keep out of the danger zone. Avoid hours of alone time in private quarters. What I mean is, stay away from houses, couches, beds, floors, tables, and for some of you, cars. Keep sex out of the conversation. We are surrounded by so much sex it's easy to get caught in sexual innuendos in everyday conversation. And trust me, conversation about sex makes you think about sex. Building good, healthy relationships means that we find a way to have intimacy, a connection, without sexual intercourse. Intimacy can come from building a closeness through communication.

Think about how much you can discover about a person when sex is not involved. Sex brings in so many emotions for both men and women. Some believe that if they engage in sex, it means exclusivity. While others have no concept of exclusiveness. And when two people are on two different pages, arguments are going to happen because of dissatisfaction. In order to maintain contentment, we must avoid those areas that bring discontentment, like premarital sex, because of our spiritual conviction or because of our emotional state and what it means to our season of singleness.

FINANCES

In this process of interviewing, I discovered that single women are either suffering financially or they are financially stable. Is there an in-between state of financial security for women? Again, this is an area that plays into your own personal conviction. What makes you feel as though you are financially secure and not on a treadmill or robbing Peter to pay Paul? God does not want us in a state of financial dismay, or he would not give us the promises of supplying our needs. Indeed, God holds true to his promises of providing for our needs. However, God expects for us to 1) put in some work, and 2) be a good steward of what he has already provided. If we are not taking care of what God has already given us, then why do we feel as though he owes us more? God does not owe us anything. In fact, he gave us more than we ever need or deserve when he sent his son, Jesus Christ.

Think about finances and how they impact contentment. Finances, whether it's a car note, student loans, a mortgage, clothes, or jewelry; are you in a position to spend like you do? Credit cards, check cashing places, and high-interest loans create additional debt that keeps us in financial disarray.

I had the most amazing time interviewing these women. We cried, we laughed, and we shared. In every woman I saw a part of me that sometimes I suppress because it's just not focused on or talked about, like the part that acknowledges that I really am single, like Chelesa and Esther, two women who hadn't focused on their singleness for years until I brought it to their attention.

I found a common bond with Joy and Tamara, as we all struggle with celibacy issues only when we are dating. Outside of that it's easy to say no. I found my commonality with Lauren, as she was raised in a single-parent household. I found commonality in Kurrean and Delilah, as they refused to pay attention to the voice of God before the marriage. I found myself in each of these women. I saw myself, as these women, thinking that I had found the man of my dreams at one point in life, but he turned out to be a nightmare.

As you read each of these stories, I pray that you can see a piece of you in every one of these women. I pray that you are honest with yourself, and realize that you are not the only one. I pray that you read each story and realize that their contentment did not come from male-bashing, but from their relationship with Christ. Their contentment is a state that brings about different emotions and feelings, but overall, they have found daily joy and satisfaction in Christ.

What I think I love most about these interviews, as well as the interviews or conversations with other ladies that helped to develop the activities in the Chapter "Working your Way to Contentment," is that none of the sessions turned negative or into male-bashing. Instead, with in each session, we, the women involved, took issues with ourselves, and not a blame game. How can we change in order to make our situation better, and that is what I recommend for you, the reader. Take a look at yourself and see what you can do differently in your own life, with your own self, your own issues, to make your situation better, to ultimately find contentment.

Just recently, I was able to witness the dismay that exists in so many women through social media. It is amazing how often I visit Facebook and see the blame game, or how often you listen to the ranting and raving of people. How often do we stop and ask, "What role I play in the situation?" I think if we asked that question—more importantly, if we asked ourselves that question, what role did I play? How did I contribute? How was I the cause?—it would cut down a lot on the blame game. In order to achieve contentment, we have to learn to take responsibility for our contribution to situations that lead to discontentment.

I point social media out because so many hide behind social media in order to point blame. For some of us, social media has become a sublet of who we are; it has replaced our true identity with a façade that allows us not to take responsibility. Women, we must take responsibility for our own actions. I have learned that over the years, I am responsible for my contentment. I am the contributing factor to achieving contentment, not my situation, not the guys I date, the work I do, or the people I associate with.

Achieving contentment means that we identify those things that lead to discontentment. In other words, achieving contentment is a personal accomplishment; no one can reach contentment for you. This is something you have to do in your relationship with Christ. You can only achieve contentment if you work to achieve contentment.

Contentment does not mean that you will not deal with thorns or have to face fears, disappointment, and discouragement. I was just hurt and disappointed only yesterday. I cried a few minutes and moped for most of the morning. However, by mid-day, I prayed and asked God to work in my life so that this would not get me down or bring me to a point of discontentment.

Contentment does not mean that we don't hurt. Contentment does not mean that we don't cry. Contentment does not mean that we do not want to be in a relationship. Contentment means that although I hurt, I know that God is on the other side of this hurt and I can make it through. I know that this hurt does not lead to me moping, complaining, or feeling sorry for myself, but helps me to grow, learn, and experience life's challenges through and in Christ.

Paul said no matter what state I am in, I am content. I am satisfied. In other words, I am satisfied with the right now. I am not running after every Tom, Dick, and Harry to try and fulfill a missing void. Although contentment is achieved through a personal goal, that doesn't mean that as women, we can't work together, stick together, and support each other. If I feel like crying because he (and I used that loosely) disappointed me again, then I cry. I call my sister friends and I cry on them. But then I am reassured through them that God will never leave me nor forsake me. It's time for us to stop getting caught in what we don't have and become content with what we do have, and that HAVE IS CHRIST.

PART III

WORKING YOUR WAY TO CONTENTMENT

To construct the Self-Assessment Contentment Survey, 13 single women from various demographics (age, race, social, economic, cultural, religious, etc.) were chosen to participate in three rounds of developing, analyzing, and discussing the survey questions. A group of five single women of various demographics (age, race, social, economic, cultural, religious, etc.) were chosen to develop and test the discussion questions for the single and group activities.

If you are unsure of how to reach contentment, section three provides a number of activities to work to your own contentment. Do these activities with a sister, a friend, or a book club.

SELF-ASSESSMENT
CONTENTMENT
EMOTIONAL SURVEY

The following questions will score your level of contentment. **Please be honest with yourself and think about your <u>whole life</u> when answering the questions.** Write the corresponding point(s) on the line.

6: Always; 5: Almost Always; 4: Often; 3; Sometimes; 2: Rarely; 1: Almost Never; 0: Never

_____ Today, would you consider your overall quality of life to be satisfying (sufficient, fulfilling, rewarding, pleasing, and enjoyable)?

_____ Would you describe yourself overall as a happy (joyful, glad, pleased) person?

_____ How often do you find yourself encouraged?

_____ How often do you find yourself unafraid of change, problems, and situations?

_____ How often do you find yourself in a state of peacefulness?

_____ How often do you find yourself joyful (in high spirits)?

_____ How often do you find yourself positive about your own life?

_____ How often are you uneasy (anxious, worried) about being single?

_____ Are you at peace with dying alone (without children or a caregiver)?

_____ Do you oftentimes find yourself happy for other couples/relationships?

_____ Do you find joy (pleased) in spending time by yourself?

_____ Do you get depressed, anxious, and/or sad when you have to spend time with others or have others around?

ADD YOUR TOTAL POINTS AND WRITE ON THE LINE BELOW

_____ Total Points

How content are you?

72-64   Always Content
63-55   Almost Always Content
54-42   Often Content
41-31   Sometimes Content
30-18   Rarely
17-9   Almost Never
8-0   Never Content

SELF-ASSESSMENT CONTENTMENT BEHAVIORAL SURVEY

The following questions will score your level of contentment. **Please be honest with yourself and think about your <u>whole life</u> when answering the questions**. Write the corresponding point(s) on the line.

6: Always; 5: Almost Always; 4: Often; 3: Sometimes;
2: Rarely; 1: Almost Never; 0: Never

_____ How often do you complain about being single?

_____ How often do you find yourself in negative conversation(s) about being single or singleness?

_____ How often do you blame others and/or situations for why you are single?

_____ How often do you partake in compulsive/excessive behaviors (i.e., overeating, overspending, shopping, drugs, alcohol)?

_____ Do you oftentimes find yourself daydreaming about what you do **NOT** have?

_____ How often have you planned your entire wedding from start to finish?

_____How often do you watch TV?

_____ How often do you lay in the bed, excluding bedtime or occasional naps?

_____ How often do you **turn down** a chance to spend time with yourself or be by yourself enjoying "me" time (i.e., movies, museum, dinner, library)?

_____ How often do you turn down date(s) with other friends/ companions?

ADD YOUR TOTAL POINTS AND WRITE ON THE LINE BELOW

_____ Total Points

How content are you?

60-54 Never Content
53-45 Almost Never Content
44-36 Rarely Content
35-25 Sometimes Content
24-16 Often Content
15-7   Almost Always Content
6-0   Always Content

IDENTIFYING YOUR THORNS (GROUP ACTIVITY OR INDIVIDUAL)

The following scenarios will assist in helping you to personally identify situations or experiences that contribute to discontentment. When reviewing the scenarios, write or discuss the first thing that comes to mind. Ask yourself, how does this make me feel? Am I happy, sad, fearful, doubtful, confused, discouraged, or disappointed? Being able to identify those triggers that create discontentment will help you counter the feelings or actions before they occur. Be HONEST when reacting to the scenarios, think about your whole life.

1. Upon arriving to church you see Lisa, John, and their children. Leaving church, you overhear Amanda and Tony with their three children discussing where they want to go for dinner. You stop by the grocery store and there is Mr. and Mrs. Jones with twins. Discuss.

2. You hear that Gina and John from church, a couple you admired, are getting a divorce.

3. A story on the news reported that a woman was discovered in her house dead after six months. It took so long to find her because her bills were being paid through automatic deduction (until the money ran out); someone had continued to cut her lawn for months.

4. You notice a significant decrease in your paycheck. After speaking with your supervisor, you are informed that in order to keep your job, you have to take a pay decrease.

5. Today, you decide to spend a few minutes on social media, only to discover numerous pictures of your friends' children.

6. Your coworker introduced you to John. John is a Christian young man, everything that you ever imagined he would be.

7. You have spent the last 18 years caring for your only child. He/she has left the nest to attend college.

8. He has called you every day for six months, spent numerous quality hours together. Suddenly he stops calling, stops texting with no explanation, no excuse.

IDENTIFYING YOUR THORNS (GROUP ACTIVITY OR INDIVIDUAL)

Review the chapter on thorns (understand this list is not exhaustive). Please be honest with yourself and/or your group mates.

1. What three (3) thorns affect your contentment?

2. What life events, changes, or situations caused these thorns?

3. Name three (3) ways you can overcome each thorn/state of discontentment.

CONTENTMENT MODEL

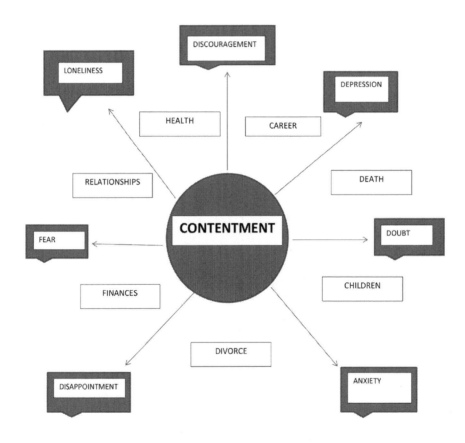

IDENTIFYING YOUR PASSION AND REACHING YOUR POTENTIAL TO ACHIEVE CONTENTMENT

The following question will help you to identify your passion(s) in life. Understand that identifying your passion can help you find contentment. Once you have begun to identify your passion, you can then begin to take steps to help you to achieve this passion, ultimately creating a source of contentment.

Make sure to be honest with yourself when answering the question and think about your whole life, not just the good or the bad parts.

If there were no obstacles in your way, what would you seek to accomplish? What would you want to do? *(Money is not an issue, time is not an issue, education is not an issue, and there are no obstacles.)*

_____

_____

_____

_____

_____

_____

_____

_____

SUGGESTED WAYS TO
REACH CONTENTMENT

- **Actively seek church membership (fellowship with the saints)**

  "Not forsaking the assembling of ourselves together, as the manner of some is; but exhorting one another: and so much the more, as ye see the day approaching" (King James Version, Hebrews 10:15).

- **Actively attend a Bible study, Sunday school, and/or life class**

  "And she had a sister called Mary, which also sat at Jesus' feet, and heard his word. But Martha was cumbered about much serving, and came to him, and said, Lord, dost thou not care that my sister hath left me to serve alone? bid her therefore that she help me. And Jesus answered and said unto her, Martha, Martha, thou art careful and troubled about many things: But one thing is needful: and Mary hath chosen that good part, which shall not be taken away from her" (King James Version, Luke 10:38-45).

- **Study and meditate on God's Word. Read your Bible <u>daily</u>. Study from a daily lesson plan/book/brochure**

   "Study to shew thyself approved unto God, a workman that needeth not to be ashamed, rightly dividing the word of truth" (*King James Version*, 2 Timothy 2:15).

- **Pray without ceasing**

- *"Pray without ceasing"* (*King James Version*, 1 Thessalonians 5:17).

- **Develop an Intimate Relationship with Christ**

   "That the God of our Lord Jesus Christ, the Father of glory, may give unto you the spirit of wisdom and revelation in the knowledge of him: The eyes of your understanding being enlightened; that ye may know what is the hope of his calling, and what the riches of the glory of his inheritance in the saints, And what is the exceeding greatness of his power to us-ward who believe, according to the working of his mighty power" (*King James Version*, Ephesians 1:17-19).

SUGGESTED WAYS TO REACH CONTENTMENT

1. Become actively invovled in a community, professional, civic organization
2. Volunteer at the food bank, clothing drive, homeless shelter
3. Volunteer at the local theater, playhouse (then you can attend events without paying and without a date)
4. Visit a local museum, art exhibit, library (there is always a tour guide so you will not be alone or feel by yourself)
5. Have a date night or date day. Go to the movies, dinner, lunch, shopping
6. Join a sports team (take swimming lessons, golf lessons, tennis lessons)
7. Join a cooking class, a cake decorating class, a pottery class, a painting class
8. Join a gym (exercise decreases stress)
9. Join a yoga class, a Zumba class
10. Take a ballroom dance class, a line dancing class
11. Travel (take a road trip)
12. Get a degree
13. Join a book club, start a book club
14. Asses your current relationship(s). Do they add or take away from who you are?
15. Set a plan (daily, monthly, and/or yearly)

16. Stop saying, "That should be me," or "That should be mine," when you see something you do not have

17. Have a girls' night (without male-bashing)

18. Host a dinner party for 2 or 3 of your friends, family

19. Take a me-cation

20. Attend a Women's Conference (Crimson Heights Ministries, Inc. is a good suggestion)

PLAN YOUR WAY TO CONTENTMENT

1. Will you work with a daily, weekly, monthly, yearly plan/calendar?

2. What resources are needed to accomplish your goal(s) (i.e., money, time, people, books)?

3. Does your plan require additional finances? If so, are you financially able to accomplish your goals? If not, seek advice to assist you with securing a budget that allows you extra activities (i.e., pay off credit card bills, pay off high mortgages).

4. Does your goal(s) require additional learning (books, degree)?

5. Is professional assistance required to achieve your goal?

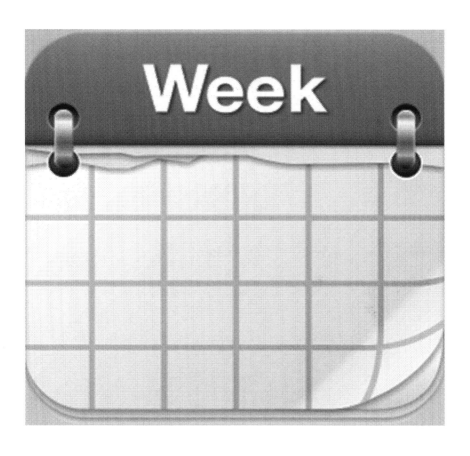

PLAN YOUR WAY TO CONTENTMENT (EXAMPLE)

GOAL: *After identifying your passion, you discover that you want to be an Oscar award-winning actor.*

It's important to remember to start with the small goals, which ultimately help you to achieve the large goal!

1. Research the business of acting
2. Research acting/training classes
3. Join a local acting class
4. Work with a local acting teacher
5. Practice daily vocal exercise
6. Take a dance class or work out with a trainer to build your endurance
7. Meet/network with local actors
8. Audition at a local theater
9. Perform at a local theater
10. Meet/Network with those living in California
11. Research the cost of living in Hollywood, California
12. Secure housing in California
13. Secure transportation to California
14. Secure work in California (who wants to be a starving artist?)
15. Audition for play, film, TV

16. Book a role in a local play
17. Join an acting class in California
18. Audition for a major motion picture
19. Shoot the film for six months
20. Win an Oscar for your portrayal of actor who leaves local city for Hollywood and scores big

Once the smaller goals are outlined, set a realistic timeline to achieve the goals.

For example, you cannot set out to move to California in August, if the class you signed up for is scheduled from May-October.

- May-October–Acting class
- October-January–Audition for local play
- January-March–Perform in local play
- March-June–Prepare to move to California (research, transportation, housing, agents, casting directors)
- July of the following year–Move to California
- August of the following year–Book a role in a movie
- February–Hear your name announced as the Oscar winner

PLAN YOUR WAY TO CONTENTMENT

MAIN GOAL:

_____

_____

_____

_____

_____

_____

_____

_____

_____

_____

_____

_____

_____

_____

_____

_____

_____

_____

_____

_____

SMALL GOAL(s):

1. _____
2. _____
3. _____
4. _____
5. _____
6. _____
7. _____
8. _____
9. _____
10. _____
11. _____
12. _____
13. _____
14. _____
15. _____
16. _____
17. _____
18. _____
19. _____
20. _____
21. _____
22. _____
23. _____
24. _____
25. _____
26. _____
27. _____
28. _____
29. _____
30. _____

$\mathcal{A}$CKNOWLEDGEMENTS

Thank you to my Lord and Savior, Jesus Christ! I sat down at the computer and I began writing two other story lines before the Holy Spirit spoke and said, "No, this is what I want you to say!" I can truly say this book is Holy Spirit-directed. I never set out to write any type of self-help book, but it's amazing when God speaks or puts things into action, they flow. This book came about with comfort and ease as I began writing, and because of that, God put the women in place who were supposed to assist with interviewing, discussions, trial and error with the surveys. And to those women I say, thank you. Thank you for your time, your talent, and your story. May God continue to use you in his service and may your story reach millions to help all women, single or married, know that there is a life of contentment in Christ.

Thank you to my petunia, my brother and my BFF; your unwavering support is what family is about. To my Buddha and Mouse, I love you unconditionally—you are what agape love truly represents. For you, Mother dear, instructed us to live by Matthew 6:33: *"But seek ye first the kingdom of God, and his righteousness; and all these things shall be added unto you."* I miss you. Donald Burton, Ruby Dunn and George Head!

And the list goes on and on—to all the family that is smiling down on me from Heaven. Angels, keep watching over me! Thank you to all immediate and extended family, so many I can't call each of you by name. Thank you to all the supporters of *Crimson Heights*, Crimson

DR. HEATHER E. BURTON

Heights Ministries, Inc. and the Crimson Experience. Thank you to my pastor emeritus, Rev. A. Charles Bowie, and the East Mt. Zion Baptist Church, for your foundational teaching in the word of God and planting a seed that continues to blossom. Thank you to my pastor, Rev. Dr. Larry W. Howard, and the Historic Greater Friendship Baptist Church, for your encouragement and support—for continuing to provide a water supply to the seed that had been planted.

Thank you to my sands, specs, and Sorors of Delta Sigma Theta Sorority, Inc. especially The Ohio State University, Epsilon Chapter and Greater Cleveland Alumnae Chapter. I thank God for sending me such great cheerleaders! As the church folk say, "If I have forgotten anyone, charge it to my head and not my heart." If God uses me to touch one person then my work is not in vain.

WORKS CITED

--American Heritage Dictionary. Boston: Houghton Mifflin Company, 1985.

--The Guideposts Family Concordance. Nashville, Tennessee: Thomas Nelson, Inc. Publishers, 1982.

--Thompson Chain Reference Bible. Kirkbridge Bible Company,

Anderson, Ken. Where to Find it in the Bible: The Ultimate A to Z Resource. Nashville, Tennessee: Thomas Nelson Publishers, 1996.

Anderson, Terry. Sermon. "When A Nation Rejects God." YouTube.com. 1 July 2013. https://www.youtube.com/watch?v=Ej46OFoSRLw

Angelou, Maya. Phenomenal Woman. New York: Random House, 1995.

Arthur, Kay. The Truth about Sex. Colorado Springs, Colorado: Water Brook Press, 2005.

Barras, Jonetta Rosa. Whatever Happened to Daddy's Little Girl? The Impact of Fatherlessness on Black Women. New York: A One World Book, The Random House Publishing Group, 2000.

Beyoncé. "Single Ladies." I Am...Sasha Fierce. New York: Columbia Records, 2008.

Bible Info.com http://www.Bibleinfo.com/en/questions/how-many-Bible-promises-are-there 2014.

Big Tymers. "Still Fly." Hood Rich. New Orleans, Louisiana: Cash Money Records, 2002.

Brainy quote. http://www.brainyquote.com/quotes/topics/
topic_inspirational.html 2014.

Bryant, T. A. Today's Dictionary of the Bible. New York: Bethany
House Publishers, 1982.

Chafin, Kenneth L. The Communicator's Commentary. Ed. Lloyd J.
Ogilvie. Waco, Texas: Word Books, 1985. 286-290.

Cleveland, James and Walker, Albertina. Please Be Patient with Me.

Cloud, Henry. Dr. How to Get a Date Worth Keeping. Grand Rapids,
Michigan: Zondervan, 2005.

Dunnam, Maxie D. The Communicator's Commentary: Galatians,
Ephesians, Philippians, Colossians, & Philemon. Ed. Ogilvie,
Lloyd J. Waco Texas. Word Books. 1982.

Farrel, Bill and Pam. Men Are Like Waffles--Women Are Like
Spaghetti: Understanding and Delighting in Your Differences.
Eugen, Oregon: Harvest House Publishers, 2001

Future. "Honest." Honest. Atlanta, Georgia: Freebandz, Epic, 19 Aug
2013.

Green, Al. "If Loving you is Wrong I don't want to be Right." If
Loving you is Wrong I don't want to be Right. KoKo Records:
1972.

Henry, Matthew. Matthew Henry's Commentary. Grand Rapids,
Michigan: Zondervan Publishing House, 1961.

Hilson, Kerri. "Get Your Money Up." In A Perfect World. Atlanta,
Georgia: Zone 4, 24 March 2009.

Hunt, T. W. The Mind of Christ: The Transforming Power of Thinking
His Thoughts. Nashville, Tennessee: B & H Publishing Group.
1995.

King James Version (KJV) http://www.Biblegateway.com/

James, Trinidad. "All Gold Everything." Don't Be S.A.F.E. New
York: Def Jam. 20 December 12.

Laymon, Charles. M, Ed. <u>The Interpreter's One-Volume Commentary on the Bible.</u> Nashville, Tennessee: Abingdon Press, 1971.

<u>Life Application Bible: New International Version</u>. Wheaton, Illinois: Tyndale House Publishers, Inc. 1991.

Madonna. "Material Girl." Like A Virgin. Burbank, California: Sire Records-Warner Brother Group, 30 Nov 1984.

Meyer, Joyce. <u>Be Anxious for Nothing: The Art of Casting Your Cares and Resting in God.</u> Fenton, Missouri: Warner Books Edition, 1998.

New International Bible (NIB)... http://www.Biblegateway.com/

Queener, John. "Plain talk about mental health: Coping with Depression and Anxiety." Wellness Workshop Wesley Temple. Wesley Temple AME Church. Akron, Ohio, 2009.

<u>The New National Baptist Hymnal: 21ˢᵗ Century Edition</u>. Nashville, Tennessee: R. H. Boyd Publishing, 2001.

<u>12 Years As A Slave</u>. Dir. Steve McQueen. Fox SearchLight Pictures and Entertainment One, 2013. 134 min.

Revised Standard Version...http://www.Biblegateway.com/

The Shirelles. "Mama Said." <u>The Shirelles Sing to Trumpets and Strings</u>. New York: Scepter. 1961.

Strong, James. LL.D., S.T.D. <u>Strong's Expanded Exhaustive Concordance of the Bible.</u> Nashville, Tennessee: Thomas Nelson Publishers, 2001.

<u>Single White Female.</u> Dir. Barbet Schroeder. Columbia Pictures, 14 August 1992. 107 min.

Vine, W. E., Unger, Merrill F. Th.M., Th.D., PhD and White, William Jr., Th.M., PhD eds. <u>Vines Complete Expository Dictionary of Old and New Testament Words</u>. Nashville, Camden, New York: Thomas Nelson, Inc. Publishers, 1985.

Walker, Hezekiah. "Grateful." <u>The Essential of Hezekiah Walker</u>. 2007

Webster's II New College Dictionary. Boston: Houghton Mifflin Company. 1999.

Wiersbe, Warren W. The Bible Exposition Commentary: An Exposition of the New Testament Comprising the Entire "BE" Series. 2 vols. Wheaton, Illinois: Victor Books, 1989.

Willmington, Dr. H. L. Willmington's Guide to the Bible. Wheaton, Illinois. Tyndale House Publishers, Inc., 1981.

Made in the USA
Columbia, SC
20 January 2022

54263551R00117